The Sufficiency of Hope

The Sufficiency
of Hope

The Conceptual
Foundations
of Religion

James L. Muyskens

Philosophical Monographs   Third Annual Series

 Temple University Press, Philadelphia

The section in Chapter 4 entitled "Kant's Moral Argument" is based on an article of the same title in *The Southern Journal of Philosophy*, Vol. XII, no. 4.

The section in Chapter 4 entitled "Life After Death: An Idle Wish or a Reasonable Hope?" is based on an article of the same title in *Philosophy Research Archives*, Vol. I, no. 1001 (1975).

The section in Chapter 4 entitled "James' Appeal to Give the Heart Its Chance" is based on an article entitled "James' Defense of a Believing Attitude in Religion" in *Transactions of the Charles S. Peirce Society*, Vol. X, no. 1 (Winter 1974).

The section in Chapter 5, "Religious-belief as Hope: Wittgensteinian Reflections" is based on an article entitled "Religious-belief as Hope" in *The International Journal for Philosophy of Religion*, Vol. V, no. 4 (Winter 1974).

Publication of this book has been assisted by a grant from the Publication Program of the National Endowment for the Humanities.

Library of Congress Cataloging in Publication Data

Muyskens, James L.   1942-
  The sufficiency of hope.

  (Philosophical monographs)
  Bibliography: p.
  Includes index.
  1. Religion—Philosophy. 2. Hope.
3. Faith. I. Title. II. Series: Philosophical
monographs (Philadelphia, 1978-) BL51.M93   200'.1   79–18714
ISBN: 0-87722-162-6

To
Jannetta Den Hartog Muyskens,
my Mother,
and the late
George Bernard Muyskens,
my Father

Say not the struggle naught availeth,
    The labour and the wounds are vain,
The enemy faints not, nor faileth,
    And as things have been things remain.

If hopes were dupes, fears may be liars;
    It may be, in yon smoke concealed,
Your comrades chase e'en now the fliers,
    And, but for you, possess the field.

For while the tired waves, vainly breaking,
    Seem here no painful inch to gain,
Far back through creeks and inlets making
    Comes silent, flooding in, the main.

And not by eastern windows only,
    When daylight comes, comes in the light,
In front the sun climbs slow, how slowly,
    But westward, look, the land is bright.

                "Say Not the Struggle Naught Availeth"
                              Arthur Hugh Clough

Hope springs eternal in the human breast;
Man never is, but always to be blessed.
The soul, uneasy, and confined from home,
Rests and expatiates in a life to come.
Lo, the poor Indian! whose untutored mind
Sees God in clouds, or hears him in the wind;
His soul proud science never taught to stray
Far as the solar walk or milky way;
Yet simple nature to his hope has giv'n,
Behind the cloud-topped hill, an humbler heav'n.

                        An Essay on Man
                        Alexander Pope

Contents

Preface

Philosophers such as Immanuel Kant and John Stuart Mill have suggested that religion be placed in the realm of hope rather than that of belief. Many philosophers of religion following Kant and Mill agree with their negative assessments of the arguments and evidence for theism. Yet the suggestion that a religious outlook be seen in terms of hope rather than belief has not been taken up in any serious way by subsequent writers, except, perhaps, by some contemporary theologians of hope. This essay is an attempt to develop and evaluate the possibility that religious commitment be placed in the realm of hope rather than that of belief.

In order to understand clearly what is meant by 'hope,' a set of necessary and jointly sufficient conditions for "S (any person) hopes that p (any proposition or event)" is constructed (Chapter I: The Structure of Hope). Following Gabriel Marcel, a special range of hopes is analyzed phenomenologically (Chapter II: The Phenomenology of Hope). Later (Chapter V) whether religious experience might be restructured as a hoping of this sort is explored.

In order to understand what is involved in the suggested retreat from belief to hope, I compare belief and hope (Chapter III: Believing and Hoping). In particular, I discuss standards of justified and/or justifiable belief and explain why—given some of these commonly accepted standards—it is a promising move to place religious-belief[1] in the realm of

xi

hope rather than ordinary belief. A position based on hope which is compatible with very strong standards of justified belief is developed. I then ask what sort of other objections could reasonably be raised against hope. With all of these possible objections in mind, I argue that the hope that God exists and the hope for life after death (two central tenets of Western theistic religions) need not fall prey to the sorts of objections which can reasonably be raised against ordinary hopes. I discuss how one who hopes that God exists and hopes for a life after death can defend his position, that is, how he can show that these *hopes* are justifiable even if it is conceded that *beliefs* that these propositions are true are not justified or justifiable (Chapter IV: The Leap Toward the Transcendent).

After I argue that such a religious position is defensible, I work out just what sort of religious view one has after making this move. Besides pointing out the features of a religion based on hope, I offer some arguments for holding that to construe religious commitment as based on hope is to have a more accurate picture of ordinary, contemporary commitment than to construe it as based on ordinary belief (Chapter V: The Venture of Religion).

Finally, I ask what a consistent theology of hope would look like and how much such a theology would have to diverge from the traditional Judeo-Christian theology of belief. The crucial differences between a theology of hope such as I present and traditional Judeo-Christian theology are pointed out in an attempt to make clear just what is at stake in choosing one in preference to the other (Chapter VI: A Theology of Hope).

This book is written as an original contribution to the field of the philosophy of religion. As such it is written with the professional philosopher in mind. However, I believe that it is important that the results of philosophical investigations not be limited to the circle of the profession but that, wherever possible, these philosophical concerns and insights be shared with the broader educated public. Hence, I address the theologian and the educated non-philosopher as well.

Note

1. It is often assumed uncritically from a look at the words that religious belief simply is a kind of belief or a subclass of beliefs differentiated from other subclasses by its subject matter. This may be the case. However, it also may be the case that—just as dry ice (frozen CO_2) is not a kind of ice (frozen H_2O)—religious belief is not a kind of belief, except in the broadest uses of the term "belief." In order not to foreclose this issue, in this work I place a hyphen between "religious" and "belief" in "religious-belief."

Acknowledgments

Of the many people to whom I owe so much, I owe my best thanks to Professor Robert M. Adams of the Philosophy Department of U.C.L.A. Without his generous help, and criticisms of earlier drafts, as well as encouragement when most needed, this book would not have been possible. There is virtually no chapter of this book that was not made better as a result of the criticisms and suggestions of Professor Allen Wood of the Sage School of Philosophy of Cornell University. Professors Nelson Pike of the University of California at Irvine, Jack Meiland and George Mavrodes of the University of Michigan, Edward Langerak of St. Olaf College, Abraham Kaplan of Tel-Aviv University, and Richard Creel of Ithaca College also read parts or all of earlier drafts, and offered useful comments and criticisms. Among my colleagues at Hunter College, I am especially grateful to Professor John Lango, for his help and encouragement; and to Professors William Bryar and Peter Caws, who read and commented on earlier drafts. Professor Joseph Margolis, as the editor of the Philosophical Monographs series, has been most helpful in the final stages of writing and revising the manuscript. This essay has benefitted greatly from his perceptive substantive and stylistic suggestions. However, none of the above named is responsible for my errors. My final thanks are to my wife, Alda, and children, Nathan and Jonathan, for their incalculable encouragement and support.

The Sufficiency of Hope

Introduction

In the *Critique of Pure Reason,*[1] Immanuel Kant places the question of the philosophical (epistemological) justification of a religious outlook in the realm of hope, "For what have we a right to hope?" John Stuart Mill, in an essay entitled *Theism*, repeats Kant's suggestion. Both Kant and Mill suggest that a religious outlook be placed in the realm of hope rather than belief. In each case, the suggestion is made after assessing the evidence for theism. These philosophers conclude that the arguments and evidence for God's existence and for such things as life after death did not provide one either with particularly good grounds for believing them or with solid ground for disbelieving them.

After Mill's negative assessment of the traditional arguments for theism, he says:

> The whole domain of the supernatural is thus removed from the region of belief into that of simple hope, and in that, for anything we can see, it is likely always to remain; for we can hardly anticipate either that any positive evidence will be acquired of the direct agency of Divine Benevolence in human destiny, or that any reason will be discovered for considering the realization of human hopes on the subject as beyond the pale of possibility.[2]

Although Kant's and Mill's suggestion to view the religious outlook in terms of hope rather than belief has not been taken up in any serious way by subsequent writers, many (perhaps most) philosophers of religion following Kant and Mill agree with their assessments. Whether a negative assessment of the arguments and evidence for theism is the correct assessment will not be dealt with in this essay. It will be assumed, however, for the sake of argument, that the arguments and evidence for and against theism do not offer either clear proof or clear disproof of the central propositions of theism.

At first glance it may appear that Kant's and Mill's suggestion to view the religious outlook in terms of hope rather than belief is *religiously* inadequate. Wouldn't the Christian, for example, be giving up far too much if he moved from the belief that the central propositions of his religion are true to the mere hope that they are true? In this study I intend to discuss just what would have to be given up as well as what would be gained if one were to follow Kant's and Mill's suggestion. Whether too much would be given up is a very complicated matter that can be decided only after careful examination of the alternatives. The final assessment cannot easily be foreseen.

Kant and Mill were moved to place the religious outlook in the realm of hope for philosophical rather than religious reasons. They could see no way to justify *believing* the central propositions of the Christian religion. Yet both felt that the religious dimension need not be denied rational or philosophically qualified persons.

Today especially with the reawakening of a sense of the need for the religious dimension in our lives and the widely accepted view that we are not rationally justified in taking as literal fact the central claims of traditional religions, we face the same problem Kant and Mill faced. As we have seen, they attempted to solve the problem by placing religion in the realm of hope instead of belief. However, neither Kant nor Mill developed the position. Development must be carried out on two fronts. It must be determined whether the view is religiously adequate, and it must be determined whether the hopes involved are justified and/or justifiable. The latter task requires that some criterion of justified and/or justifiable hope be established.

Mill says that the question of a criterion for justified or justifiable hopes has not been developed but that it is a very important issue to which philosophers should address themselves. Hopes like those of the religious outlook, for which there can be no expectation of probable grounds, Mill places in the "region of imagination." Lamenting the fact that philosophers have not developed guidelines for the proper employment of the imagination, he says:

> The principles which ought to govern the cultivation and the regulation of the imagination—with a view, on the one hand, of preventing it from disturbing the rectitude of the intellect and the right direction of the actions and will, and, on the other hand, of employing it as a power for increasing the happiness of life and giving elevation to the character—are a subject which has never yet engaged the serious consideration of philosophers, though some opinion on it is implied in almost all modes of thinking on human character and education.[3]

I intend to develop a criterion for justified hopes. With it I shall ask whether it would be rational to hope—and whether one would be justified in hoping—for such things as God's existence and life after death, central tenets of the traditional Judeo-Christian religious outlook.

Although Kant and Mill made their suggestions many years ago, neither they nor subsequent philosophers of religion have followed through on the suggestions. Hence, in order to advance in this area, some careful groundwork must be laid. The first two chapters of the essay—"The Structure of Hope" and "The Phenomenology of Hope"—are attempts to provide the required foundation. In subsequent chapters we shall contrast criteria for justified hope and for justified belief and explore the other issues mentioned.

Besides the suggestions made by Kant and Mill a recent development in theology points to the possibility of construing hope as providing the cognitive basis for a religious outlook. Within the last fifteen years, many theologians have come to identify themselves with a movement called "the theology of hope." One group within this class is especially interested in biblical exegesis. Their thesis is that hope is the central motif of the primary Christian literature. They suggest that "hope" ought to be the focal point of Judeo-Christian theology.[4] Other theologians of hope have more of an apologetic and philosophical interest. They maintain that it is part of human nature to hope. The experience of hope opens one up to the religious, the transcendent. Hence it is suggested that a theological treatise or a discussion of the religious needs of man should begin with hope. Gabriel Marcel clearly is the best spokesman for this position. (Some of Marcel's examples and arguments are to be examined below.)

Another divergent group of theologians that can be fit under the umbrella of the theology of hope are the so-called radical theologians who have found, on the one hand, that they lack the gift of faith, where faith is understood more or less as the acceptance (without scruple) of a body of doctrines which are taken to be indubitably revealed by God, and, on the other hand, that the "death of God" theology as well as the various forms of humanism are empty and unsatisfactorily express their concern.[5] William Hamilton, one of the "death of God" theologians, once wrote that "the theologian today and tomorrow is a man without faith, without hope, with only the present, with only love to guide him."[6] The theologian of hope in this third group would see Hamilton as having moved too far. He would agree that the "theologian today and tomorrow" does not have the gift of faith but he would say that he has hope as well as love to guide him. The questions such a theologian poses are: Why should I give up hope even if I cannot fathom faith? Can a religiously acceptable position be formulated on the basis of hope rather than faith?

1 The Structure of Hope

In order to be clear as to what hope is, it is useful to begin by considering how we use the word "hope." Hence, I want to examine first several classic analyses of the concept. With the help of these, an adequate philosophical or logical analysis[1] will be presented. That is, it will be argued that the necessary conditions (and perhaps the jointly sufficient conditions) of hope have been found.

Hume on Hope

Turn first to David Hume's discussion of hope in Book II of the *Treatise.*[2] Hope, according to Hume, is one of the "direct passions." Hope and its opposite, fear, are the most important of the "direct passions." The other "direct passions" are desire and aversion, joy and grief. The "direct passions" are those emotions[3] which arise immediately and naturally from the perception of some good or evil. (Good and evil are in turn defined in terms of pleasure and pain.) It is a human propensity to move toward the good and to shun the evil. When good is certain Hume says that *joy* is produced. When evil is certain *grief* or sorrow arises. If good is uncertain the situation gives rise to *hope*. If evil is uncertain the situation gives rise to *fear*. In short, Hume is picturing a probability continuum with joy and grief at the extremities and hope and fear lying somewhere in between. When the scale tips toward the good prospect one is hopeful (he has more joy than grief); and when the scale of evidence tips toward the bad prospect one is fearful (one is more sorrowful than joyful).

Hume gives the following account of the mental processes involved.[4] Confronted with contrary chances for a particular event's occurring, the mind is incessantly tossed from one consideration to another. At one moment it focuses on favorable evidence and the next moment it focuses on unfavorable evidence. In those cases in which the event is the object of attraction (or is the object of aversion), the moment the mind focuses on the evidence in favor of the event occurring one experiences momentary joy (or sorrow).

In considering a possible event whose occurrence is uncertain, one experiences, then, these numerous flashes of the contrary emotions[5] of joy and sorrow. It is the union of these contrary emotions which produces the emotions of hope and fear. If the experiences of joy dominate, we call the emotional state one of hope. On the other hand, if the experiences of sorrow dominate, one is in a state of fear.

Hume's "proof" of his position[6] is an appeal simply to consider what happens when probabilities are increased or decreased. By merely adding and subtracting probabilities, he claims, the appropriate emotional state changes from joy to hope to fear to grief and *vice versa*. Hume says that this "proof" is analogous to proofs provided in optics and that no stronger proofs could be given.

Based on the above considerations, Hume offers the following logical (or philosophical) analysis of "hope" and "fear": "S (a person) hopes that p (where p stands for a proposition or event)" if and only if (1a) "p is good (that is, p is an object of attraction)" and (1b) "p is probable." "S fears that p" if and only if (2a) "p is evil (that is, p is an object of aversion)" and (2b) "p is probable."[7]

A shortcoming of Hume's logical analyses of "hope" and "fear" that immediately comes to mind is that what one hopes for need only be *considered* to be good and to be probable. It need not be good and probable. The value judgment and the probability estimate are "person relative."

Condition (1a) also requires some clarification. Most classical writers on the emotions including Hume use the contrasting notions of "good" and "evil." However, the connotations of these notions have changed considerably since the eighteenth century. "Good" today often means "morally good" or at least has moral connotations. Contrasting notions such as "desirable" and "undesirable" are perhaps better. Hume's condition, then, should read: (1a′) "p (the object of hope) is desirable (to S)." Not only does this capture more accurately the intent of the classical writers, but the contrasting terms "desirable" and "undesirable" (although there may be difficulties and ambiguities with these terms as well) provide a more plausible analysis of emotions such as hope.[8] It is obvious that some condition such as the revision of (1a) is necessary. If a person hopes for something, then he or she must desire it, or want it to be the case, or judge it favorably in some respect.

If (1a′) is a necessary condition, is "p is considered *probable*" (1b′) also necessary? If we say "p is probable," no doubt we mean that the odds for p are 50 per cent or better. However, it is certainly the case that people hope for things even when the odds are, so to speak, against them, i.e., less than 50 per cent. For example: "I hope for John's recovery even though the medical experts have said that his chances are very slim." Hence, (1b′) cannot be a necessary condition. People hope for p when p has any degree of probability between (but not including) 0 and 1.

An additional problem is that condition (1b′) is ambiguous. It does not make clear what mental processes a person must go through. Is an *estimation* of probability a necessary condition of hope? Is it enough if a person simply has certain beliefs about the prospects of that for which he hopes? Or must he go through a process of calculating the prospects? It is this latter interpretation that corresponds with Hume's.

In a recent article entitled "Hope," an English philosopher, J. P. Day, also accepts (1b′) with the interpretation that in hoping one makes probability estimates.[9] However, the condition thus interpreted is too strong. It is not neces-

sary that one actually make probability estimates or judg-
ments concerning the object of one's hope in order to be
hoping. In fact, in some clear cases (to be discussed below, in
the chapter titled "The Phenomenology of Hope") one
who hopes may simply refuse to make probability estimates.
In such cases one does not weigh factors which are taken to
be evidence *pro* and *con*.

The fact that people who are philosophically and scientifically quite unsophisticated are at least as capable of hoping
as are "more enlightened" folk also lends support to the
claim that the estimation of probabilities is not a necessary
condition of hope. Except in a very watered-down sense of
the phrase, many unsophisticated people who hope do not
estimate or calculate probabilites. In most cases even sophisticated people do not consciously calculate evidence; they
simply hope. If challenged they may calculate the odds and
produce reasons for their hope—although the reasons provided as a result of reflection and calculation will very likely
not be the ground upon which their hope was originally
based.

On the strength of these considerations, condition (1b′)
might be better stated as follows: "Neither p nor not-p is
certain for S."

We have made some progress in trying to understand what
it is to hope. We have two strong candidates for necessary
conditions, namely, "S desires that p" and "Neither p nor
not-p is certain for S." Before we continue our search with
the help of Hobbes' and Descartes' analyses of "hope," it
may, given Hume's account, be useful to look at the "geogra-
phy" of hope. This relatively simple account of the relationship of hope to certain other emotions or dispositions should
be helpful later. As we have seen, according to Hume, hope is
to be analyzed in terms of an object which is desired and a
high probability estimate. In fear, the object is repugnant or
an object of aversion and the probability estimate is high.
There are two other logically possible combinations of these
two elements that Hume does not consider. We could have:

    I.   Object of desire and high probability estimate
   II.   Object of desire and low probability estimate
  III.   Object of aversion and high probability estimate
  IV.   Object of aversion and low probability estimate

Hume considers only I (hope) and III (fear). According to Hume, III is *the* contrary of I.[10] But why aren't II and IV also contraries of I? Or why isn't II said to be *the* contrary of I instead of III? In order to treat II in emotional terms let us take it to be a partial logical analysis of "despair." (I will revise the analysis later. But it is close enough to the correct analysis to do for now.) If a person has just made his probability estimate and *discovers* that the object to which he has an aversion has a low probability (as in IV), his state of mind may be described as one of relief. That which threatened his sense of security and well-being has faded into the background. Very roughly, IV may be taken as a (partial) logical analysis of "security." A person feels secure when that toward which he has an aversion does not appear to be a real possibility or threat. It is the relations between hope and despair and hope and security rather than hope and fear that are of the most importance for the subsequent issues of this essay.

Hobbes and Descartes on Hope

Hobbes calls hope an "appetite with an opinion of attaining."[11] Despair is an appetite without an opinion of attaining. Fear is "aversion with opinion of hurt from the object." "Appetite" and "aversion" are understood by Hobbes in terms of approach and avoidance or attraction and repulsion. To have an appetite for something is simply to have an attraction for it. That toward which one is attracted is good and that from which one is repulsed evil.

René Descartes says that when "we consider whether there is much or little prospect that we shall obtain what we desire, that which represents to us that there is much probability of this excites in us hope, and that which represents to us that there is little, excites fear."[12] Extreme fear becomes despair.

The logical analysis of "hope" on Hobbes' account is very similar to Hume's. "S hopes that p" if and only if (3a) "S is attracted to p (or, synonymously, S considers p to be good)," and (3b) "S considers p to be likely." Hobbes' condition (3a) comes to the same thing as Hume's condition (1a).

Hobbes' condition (3b) is different from Hume's (1b′). According to Hobbes the estimating of probabilities is *not* included. He simply states that one must have "an opinion of attaining." In this respect, if our earlier criticism is correct, Hobbes' analysis is superior to Hume's.

The most accurate restatement of Hobbes' rather quaint phrase "with an opinion of attaining" would be either (i) "S believes that p is more probable than not" or (ii) "S expects that p." (i) and (ii) are roughly synonymous. One would not expect an event to occur if he considered its probability to be less than 50 per cent. If one judged that the probability of an event occurring is at least 50 per cent or better he would expect it to occur. Clearly this is a stronger condition than that the object of hope is considered to be possible (in the sense that it is considered not to be impossible).

If by "S has an opinion of attaining p" Hobbes means "S believes that p is more probable than not," the condition is too strong for reasons similar to those indicated before. Consider the following examples: If there is merely a chance that I will make it to shore after my boat has capsized and sunk, very likely I still hope to manage to do it. If there is the least reason to believe that miners trapped a thousand feet below in a caved-in coal mine might still be alive, we normally continue our rescue efforts *with the hope that* they are alive. We do not normally say, "We expect that they are alive." Nor do we say, "We would very much like it if they were alive." We say, "We hope that they are alive."

Consider the following case: After visiting a woman whose husband has what has been diagnosed by his physicians as terminal cancer one might say, "She hopes against hope that her husband will recover." Less colorfully what is being asserted is that, although she realizes that the odds (so to speak) are very much against her, she continues to hope that her husband will recover. She hopes in the face of overwhelming odds. Perhaps such behavior is irrational (the notion of reasonable hopes will be discussed later), but it is rather common behavior—and is correctly called hope.

Very likely the woman in the example does *not expect* her husband's recovery. She desires his recovery and believes it to fall within the realm of possibility. Very likely she will be looking for signs of recovery, but she need not therefore shut her eyes to clear indications that her husband's condition is worsening. If one were so cruel as to ask her if she expected her husband to recover, her response might well be: "No, I guess I don't expect it, but I do *hope* for it." Expectation is not a necessary condition of hoping.

If the above criticism of Hobbes is correct concerning his condition (3b), the same criticisms apply to Descartes' analysis. On Descartes' account one hopes for something only when the probability of it is considered to be great (high). It has been argued that the probability need not be high. That for which one hopes simply must be possible (or in some degree probable).

A contemporary philosopher, J. M. O. Wheatley,[13] follows Hobbes and Descartes in considering *expectation* to be a necessary condition for hoping; he says that in cases in which one "has no expectation of its fulfillment" to say someone hopes "would be a misuse of the word 'hope.'" Wheatley considers cases of expectation of some event to be cases in which the probability of that event is taken to be greater than 50 per cent. Unfortunately, Wheatley does not make it clear why saying that one hopes for something even when he does not expect it is a misuse of language. It appears that Wheatley makes this claim on the assumption that Hobbes' analysis is correct. However, as we have seen, that analysis is incorrect. It imposes too strong a condition on hope.

Of course, a person *can*—and, no doubt, some people do—give up hope in situations when the chances of success are less than fifty-fifty or when one no longer expects the favorable possibility. Poor odds may be sufficient for one to give up hope or to lose hope. The point here is simply that one need not. There are numerous clear cases of hope in the face of formidable odds (such as those mentioned above). In actuality, the point at which one gives up hope differs from case to case and person to person. But if we speak of hope in general (as in looking for the necessary conditions for "*S* hopes that   *p*") no more can be required than that *p* be logically or causally possible. What *is* necessary is that the object of hope be considered neither impossible nor inevitable (for example, logically entailed by some known proposition). In other words, there must be *uncertainty* concerning the occurrence of that for which one hopes (if it is an event) or concerning the truth of that about which one hopes (if it is a proposition). Hobbes', Descartes', and Wheatley's analyses of "hope" are too restrictive in ruling out cases in which the chances are merely considered to be very slim.

Hobbes' and Descartes' analyses, however, are also too inclusive. Although they fail to notice the fact, there is an upper limit to the probability estimate that one can make and still hope. It is part of the force of Hume's analysis that, as he points out, once we are certain we go beyond hope to something better, namely, joy. Such certainty entails that we are more than hopeful.

The analyses of "hope" so far discussed posit too stringent a cognitive condition—namely, that *S* must consider *p* to be probable or likely or that *S* must expect *p*. Since so many capable philosophers have maintained this (erroneous) position, perhaps we should consider whether an important insight is being misleadingly or inaccurately expressed therein. Consider that an agent who hopes acts in large part like a person who actually believes that the object of his hopes is real. Hoping for something involves practical consequences and entails certain actions or dispositions to act. One who hopes for *p* arranges his life and emotions as if *p* were the case. Still we must distinguish the practical dispositions linked with hope and with actual cognitive expectation. If one hopes that *p* one is *disposed to act as if p*. Hence, the actions of the person who hopes for *p* may be very similar to those of the person who expects (or believes) that *p*; but it does not follow that the person hoping that *p* expects that *p*.

Aquinas on Hope

One of the most interesting analyses of "hope" is to be found in St. Thomas' discussion of the emotions in the *Summa Theologiae*.[14] According to St. Thomas, "*S* hopes that *p*" if and only if:

(4a) "*p* is good"
(4b) "*p* is in the future"
(4c) "*p* is attainable only with difficulty"
(4d) "*p* is possible."[15]

Each of these conditions must be examined separately and necessary corrections and revisions made. We begin with (4a). Condition (4a)—given the discussion above as well as the argument below—should read: (4a') "*S* desires *p*." Whether *p* is actually good (morally good, prudentially good, technically good, or whatever) is not the issue. What is important (as was pointed out in Hume's analysis) is not whether what is hoped for is good according to some supposed objective criterion, but whether it is desired or wanted (and thus considered good) by the person hoping.

Condition (4b), "*p* is in the future," is simply invalid. That for which one hopes need not be in the future; it may be in the present or the past as well. This can be readily shown by counter examples. One may say for example: (i) "I hope that they are having good weather in Washington for the game today." Or: (ii) "I hope that she is well again now." Or: (iii) "I hope that I wasn't an embarrassment to the host at the party last night." Or: (iv) "I hope they finally had rain in Phoenix." Here we have cases of one hoping for something in the present ((i) and (ii)) and in the past ((iii) and (iv)).[16]

Condition (4b) gains plausibility perhaps not only because many or most of our hopes are future oriented but also, as was indicated earlier, because we cannot hope for what we take to be certain. A person cannot hope that his team won the race yesterday if he is sure that it did. A person cannot hope that his brother is well again if he knows that he is well now. Much of what is past or present is certain for us. We can only hope that someone is well again if for some reason—say, separation at some distance—we cannot directly see whether he is well, or have only a report which we believe without conclusive evidence to be reliable, or the like. A necessary condition of hoping is some degree of relevant ignorance regarding that for which we hope. Most of what is in the future is uncertain, to some degree we are ignorant about the future. "Who knows what tomorrow will bring?" But clearly not everything in the past or present is certain; provided no other necessary condition is violated, we can (logically), and in fact we do, hope for things in the past or present as well as in the future.

Aquinas' condition, therefore, concerning the futurity of that for which we hope is by no means necessary. What he apparently wished to capture by (4b) is completely covered by the condition (introduced earlier): "Neither p nor not-p is certain for S."

Condition (4c), namely, "p is attainable only with difficulty" has not been encountered before. Aquinas says:

> Thirdly, it [the object of hope] must be something arduous, attainable only with difficulty: we do not speak of hoping for a trifle which lies easily within our grasp. In this way hope differs from desire or longing which have for their object a future good without qualification.[17]

But Aquinas' constraint is too stringent. I may, for instance, hope that it will not rain for the picnic tomorrow. Such a state of affairs is not brought about by anyone—*a-fortiori*, it is not brought about with difficulty by me or anyone else.

Although condition (4c) is untenable, it does point to a distinction regarding the analysis of "hope" which I intend to develop in the next chapter. If "attained with difficulty" were understood to include things wholly or almost wholly beyond one's power, hopes that met condition (4c) would be philosophically and theologically the most interesting cases. This range of peculiarly profound hopes may be set aside as warranting special study. But our initial task is to give an account of the concept of "hope," in general. Hence, it would be inappropriate to adopt as a necessary condition any constraint applying to some hopes but not to others.

Another noteworthy feature of Aquinas' discussion is that (4c) is advanced as the condition distinguishing hoping from wishing and longing. Aquinas quite correctly points out that hoping is qualified in a way that wishing is not.

There are at least three important ways in which hoping is distinguished from wishing. (1) One can wish (counterfactually) that he had not taken a particular job or that he had chosen a different profession. But, logically, one cannot hope counterfactually. A person may consistently say, "I wish to marry a prince. But I know that it is not possible." But the following would be inconsistent: "I hope to marry a prince. But I know that it is not possible." Hoping has a possibility condition that wishing does not have. (2) Hoping has a closer relation to action or dispositions to act than does wishing. The person who hopes that p acts as if p were true. He arranges his life and his emotions as if he believed that p. An inclination to act as if one believed that p is not entailed by wishing that p (since one may wish counterfactually). (3) If hoping and wishing are both analyzed in terms of desire, wishing covers a much larger range than hoping. One can wish for things that he would not desire on balance. Yet one does not hope for such things. Consider the case of a person who, for reasons of health, has quit smoking. Typically, such a person both desires to smoke and not to smoke. On the one hand, he desires not to take up the habit again, and, on the other, he strongly desires (wishes) to have a cigarette. In such a case, it could be said of the man that he hopes that he will refrain from smoking, i.e., that his desire to kick the habit will overcome his desire to have a cigarette. It could not normally be said of such a man that, wishing to smoke a cigarette, he hopes he will smoke one. What is hoped for, in this case, is the object of the overriding desire.

Of course, there are many cases of hoping in which such clear-cut warring desires do not obtain. Our examples may not be entirely representative. Certainly, there are cases in which people hope, and yet engage in no reflection at all concerning preferred alternatives. So it would be too strong a condition to hold that what is hoped for must be desired or preferred on balance, the object of an overriding desire. What is brought out by the example of the man who quit smoking is that one cannot hope for something (p) if some alternative incompatible with it (p) is preferred on balance by that person. (In such cases, the desire that p cannot form the basis for a hope that p.)

Not everything that is desired and that is considered neither impossible nor inevitable can be hoped for. As in the passage cited above, Aquinas maintains that the objects of hope are qualified or restricted in a way that the objects of longing or desire are not. We have been trying to identify the required restriction. One can long, or wish, for something that he knows is not preferred on balance. But one does not hope for such a thing. If one hopes for something (p), it cannot be the case that he would say, "I do not prefer p on balance." If S hopes for p, either S prefers p on balance or S believes that he does not prefer anything that opposes his desire for p. The following formulation of this necessary condition is most perspicuous: "It is not the case that p is not preferred by S on balance, or that S believes that q, which he prefers on balance, is incompatible with p."

On the basis of the above discussion we have the following set of necessary conditions for "S hopes that p."

(5a) "S desires that p."
(5b) "It is not the case that p is not preferred by S on balance, or that S believes that q, which he prefers on balance, is incompatible with p."
(5c) "Neither p nor not-p is certain for S."
(5d) "S is disposed to act as if p."

Are conditions (5a) - (5d) jointly sufficient? I believe that they are. That is, I believe that we have a set of conditions equivalent to "S hopes that p." However, the notion of "hope" is not only very broad—including profound hopes of the sort to be discussed in the next chapter, as well as very mundane ones—but its borders are vague as well. There are bound to be differences of opinion concerning whether borderline cases are cases of hoping or of wishing or entertaining or believing or imagining, etc.

Fortunately, we need not refine our logical analysis of "hope" further, since, for what follows, what is crucial is not whether the set of conditions proposed are jointly sufficient; it is, rather, whether what we have claimed to be necessary conditions have been established as such.

2 The Phenomenology of Hope

Some Cases of Hope

The discussion in this chapter of certain especially interesting and clear-cut examples of experiences of hoping is based on Gabriel Marcel's treatment of hope.[1] Specific cases of hoping for something[2] will be examined in order to see just what the "ingredients" of such experiences are. Following Marcel, we may say that a person cannot directly determine whether the analysis of the experience of hope is correct— that is, whether the "ingredients" found are the essential ones—unless he has had an experience of a certain favored type. This is why Marcel says at the outset of his article, "Sketch of a Phenomenology and a Metaphysics of Hope," that he appeals "to a special experience which it must be supposed you have."[3]

Marcel does not refer us to any canonical literature of hope experiences. To a large extent he appears to rely on his own experience. He feels, moreover, that the experience is a rather common one. Hence, we are to suppose that we have ample material upon which to draw. However, as will be evident with the unfolding of the phenomenological account, if it is correct, then it is quite likely that the number of people who have experiences of the profound sorts of hoping under consideration here must be diminishing in our technological society.

Of course, if a person has not had such paradigmatic experiences of hoping, he can still examine the reports of others and determine the "ingredients" of such an experience. But one of the basic tests of adequacy of a phenomenological treatment of this kind—namely, does the account ring true to my own experience?—obviously is not available to the person who has not had the experience.

In short, in following Marcel, what we are to ask is: Of what does the experience of hoping in its most profound instances consist? The answer to be given is to be of the type which is given *from out of the perspective of the experiencer.*

The cases of hoping that Marcel deals with have been twice referred to as paradigmatic cases. Marcel himself does not use this terminology. However, throughout his discussion, he obviously focuses on a few selected cases because he takes them to be representative of genuine or fundamental hope. These are "hard-core" as opposed to borderline cases, which are barely distinguishable from cases of liking or wishing or expecting, etc. They are paradigm cases of hope. However, not only do they have features common to all cases properly described as hoping, they also have certain special features that they do not share with the common cases. Since this special range of hope is of the greatest interest for our present purpose, we should look at these cases not so much for what is revealed about all cases of hope but for what is revealed about certain profound, personally commiting, hopes.

The following are the paradigmatic cases of "I hope . . ." most often referred to by Marcel in his various discussions.

(i) I am bed-ridden by an illness which might paralyze me for life. I hope for the freedom of movement which would come with a restoration of health.

(ii) A loved one is seriously ill. I hope for his recovery.

(iii) I am in (say) a Nazi concentration camp. I hope for deliverance.

(iv) I am separated from my family (say by war) but I hope to be reunited with them.

(v) My country is occupied by enemy troops. I hope for deliverance.

It is significant to note that in the description of each example the situation of the person who hopes is given. The situation has an important bearing on the strength and type of response. To use Marcel's expression, in the cases cited, the person appears to himself to be "in captivity." He finds himself imprisoned, pinned in, in darkness, lost, in need. A door through which he wants to pass has been closed. Furthermore, the person who hopes finds himself in a situation in which he feels that he cannot rise "to a certain fullness of life" unless that for which he hopes is realized. That is, the person believes that something integral to his well-being or full life is denied him unless the hope is realized. In short, in these cases, the person who hopes has been thrust into what can best be described as a *tragic* situation, from which he sees no easy or ready escape.

Another in the same situation may feel hopeless or be without hope. To be without hope does not mean that one has no hopes. It means that one has no hopes of a certain sort. Imagine a person of whom we would say he is (absolutely) without hope or feels utterly hopeless. A clear candidate might be an elderly person who contemplates suicide in order (say) to terminate an illness.[4] Such a person may hope that his son will provide for his widow (the son's mother); he may hope that he will have no visitors tonight; he may hope that the horse on which he bet his last $10 will win; he may hope that his suicide attempt will not fail and will appear to be an accident; and so on. Yet he is without hope, for *he* does not want to face the future such as he expects it to be. For *him*, all hope is gone. He is willing to close the door to any further possibilities for his own future or self-development. He no longer has the confidence that he is, or the hope that he will be, the kind of person he wanted to be or thought that he ought to be.

In the examples of hoping listed above, each of which has a tragic context, attainment of the object of hope is seen as integrally tied up with the person's concept of himself and/or his potential for fulfillment. Cases of hoping in non-tragic contexts either would not, or would not be seen to, be so closely linked to the fulfillment, happiness, development, or survival of a hopeful person.

Hope that is integrally related to self-fulfillment is most clearly exhibited in examples that obtain in tragic contexts, in situations in which one sees oneself in a state of captivity. Recall that wanting something is a necessary condition for hoping for it. Also, relevant wants must be seen as not inconsistent with the promotion of the individual's welfare. No doubt the most vivid and clear-cut cases of a person having vital wants, i.e., wants integrally connected with his welfare, are cases in which a person sees himself as being (finds himself) in a tragic situation. So we have the most intense wants of the appropriate kind in the cases cited.

This is not to deny the possibility of having equally intense desires in situations in which there are good prospects that what one wants will obtain. The point is that when one cannot rely on good odds for a desired possibility, he must, if he is to hope for it, hope on the strength of his desire. Conversely, if one persists in hoping in a tragic situation, this must be due to his strong desire. This need not be the case in non-tragic situations. For example, Alice and Bill may want to get married; they meet no obstacles in achieving this desire. Romeo and Juliet may also want to get married, but their parents strongly object; they decide to go ahead with their marriage plans anyway. Alice's and Bill's desires may be just as strong as Romeo's and Juliet's. But they need not be so in order to succeed. And even if their desires to marry are just as strong, they are not as vividly demonstrated as they are in Romeo and Juliet's case.

Marcel believes it to be an empirical fact that when human existence "appears as a captivity it becomes so to speak subject to hope."[5] Such situations *invite* the exercise of hope. Marcel also says that "as a matter of fact, the general condition of man, even when his life appears to be quite normal, is always that of a captive, by reason of the enslavements of all kinds which he is called upon to endure, if only on account of the body, and more deeply still because of the night which shrouds his beginning and his end."[6] He wonders whether "in the last analysis hope might not always be looked on as an active reaction against a state of captivity. It may be that we are capable of hoping only in so far as we start by realizing that we are captives."[7]

It is rather doubtful that a psychologically necessary condition of hoping is that one realize that he is a "captive." Certainly it would be difficult to establish the general thesis. Paradigmatic cases such as those listed above are, however, active reactions against a state of captivity. As has been argued, this feature brings out vividly the element of personal resolve involved in hope. It is a matter of record, furthermore, that hope is most intensely affirmed in the face of experiences (such as death) that seem to close one in completely or to spell utter defeat. Many have had experiences in which life, or some aspect of life, appears tragic or pointless, only to find that they cannot help but interject that tragedy need not be the final word. They feel, so to speak, compelled to remain open to the possibility of an additional word. They feel compelled to hope.[8]

If situations like those of our examples invite the exercise of hope, clearly not everyone finds that they demand such a response. Other alternatives arise. For instance, there is the possibility either (i) of acceptance of the present (tragic) situation as binding or final, or (ii) of non-acceptance.[9]

Those who come down on the side of accepting the tragic situation as final have several quite different options open to them. Consider some familiar responses. One can, accepting a situation as "a certain *fatum*," *capitulate*—that is, one can "go to pieces under this sentence," one can "disarm before the inevitable."[10] The "option" of surrender before what one takes to be inevitable and disastrous Marcel calls despair. However, one need not, accepting the situation as "a certain *fatum*," capitulate or surrender. One can stand his ground resolving that the *fatum* will not ruin him, will not destroy his integrity. Such a position of resignation was taken by the Stoics—or at least it is the position they advocated.

In contrast to despair and resignation, one may hope in such a situation, one may be unwilling to accept the tragic situation as final. Such a person is determined to let time open up new possibilities.[11] He keeps the door open; hoping, he resolves that tragedy will not be the final word. He commits himself to an outlook which provides for the possibility that what must obtain to dislodge the present finality will obtain. Since what he hopes for must remain uncertain, despair remains a constant and strong temptation.[12]

This non-acceptance of the finality of the present situation is not simply negative. It is not merely a revolt. It is an affirmation not unlike that often made by the late Robert F. Kennedy during the 1968 Presidential campaign: "We can do better." Marcel compares this attitude of non-acceptance with the attitude of a person who is patient with another.[13] Even though Bill's present actions are disappointing (Bill is an alcoholic), when Alice (his wife) is patient with him, she is unwilling to say that he is good for nothing or incurable. She respects his independence, i.e., she sees that his having aspirations does not insure success, and she realizes that if Bill is to improve or change, he must do so on his own time. She sees each new moment as pregnant with possibilities. She does not accept her husband's present behavior as a true indication of his final condition. Although she cannot effect the desired change, she resolves that the improvement may occur in due course.

The example just given may be somewhat misleading: it suggests that hope belongs only to the patient and the conservative, not to the revolutionary. But surely, not merely the patient and the conservative can hope. The point of the example is to rule out a certain type of non-acceptance. Ruling this out hardly yields the conclusion that only the patient hope.

We can get at just what type of non-acceptance Marcel feels must be ruled out by looking at cases we describe as cases of acting in desperation or desperately. Being desperate is different from (or perhaps a special case of) being in despair. It is certainly different from being resigned to one's fate. In a certain sense, desperation is both non-acceptance and acceptance of the finality of the situation, whereas resignation is solely acceptance.

Consider the following case in which resignation, despair, desperation, and hope are compared: Matthew, Mark, Luke and John are stranded in the desert without necessary provisions. Matthew gives up and *resigns* himself to death in the desert. Mark *despairs* of saving his life. Both Matthew and Mark do nothing to save their lives because they believe that no such activity will save their lives. Luke, on the other hand, is *desperate* concerning the saving of his life. Being desperate, he is disposed to do anything within his power to bring about his safety. Yet Luke does *not* believe that he will save his life. In one sense, Luke accepts the situation as final, but in another, he does not. Roughly speaking, Luke accepts the situation *cognitively* as final, but *emotionally* he cannot. Mark, who despairs, also cognitively accepts the situation as final and cannot do so emotionally. In contrast to Mark and Luke, who emotionally cannot accept the situation as final, Matthew (who has resigned himself to his fate) accepts the situation as final both cognitively and emotionally. However, Mark's and Luke's emotional refusals issue in different forms of behavior: for Mark (who despairs), no action to bring about a change in the situation; for Luke (who is desperate), frantic action to bring about a change. John (in contrast to Matthew and Mark) hopes and (in common with Luke) is disposed to do whatever is within his power to bring about his own safety. But, in contrast to Luke, John is both cognitively and emotionally unwilling to accept the tragic situation as final. The non-acceptance favored by the desperate person is not sufficient for the person who hopes. One element of hope, then, is *non-acceptance* of the present tragic situation as final. This is not only an emotional unwillingness to accept the present plight but a firm conviction that the tragedy in which the person who hopes finds himself need not be the final word.

Hope and Optimism

We may probe more deeply our special range of hope experiences by returning to Marcel's account. Marcel distinguishes between being hopeful and being optimistic. Although the expressions ("I am hopeful" and "I am optimistic . . .") are often used interchangeably, they are here used in a more technical sense. Actually even in ordinary usage, subtle differences are registered between being hopeful and being optimistic. But they are not often required, and so these expressions usually replace one another without confusion.

What Marcel is trying to uncover are two quite different orientations toward life: HOPE (that is, the special range of profound hope outlined in the previous section) and optimism. These two approaches to life are found prominently in the religious setting, but we shall examine them more generally. HOPE will be explored later as a specifically religious outlook.

Marcel says that the difference between HOPE and optimism "is a difference which may seem to be more of a musical than a logical order."[14] If I understand him correctly, what he means is that, although the expressions "I am hopeful . . ." and "I am optimistic . . ." could very well be given quite similar logical analyses, there is a fundamental *phenomenological* difference between the two. That is, similar formal conditions must obtain in order either to hope or to be optimistic that something will occur, i.e., the same object must be considered possible, desirable, etc. Still, there is a difference in feeling and in the way things appear to one in HOPING and in being optimistic. What is the difference? Marcel says that the optimist "relies upon an experience which is not drawn from the most intimate and living part of himself, but, on the contrary, is *considered from a sufficient distance* to allow certain contradictions to become alternated or fused into a general harmony."[15] On the other hand, HOPE is drawn from "the most intimate and living part" of oneself.

The optimist can best be pictured as a *spectator* having particularly keen sight. He can (or at least he believes he can) see—more clearly than others—both what is desirable in the long run and the relevant facts signifying that the desirable will obtain. "If your vision is as good as mine you are bound to see that such and such"—this is the (tacit) claim of the optimist. Examples of such optimism are: Leibniz's theodicy,[16] Teilhard de Chardin's Christian metaphysics, many economists' statements concerning an end to the inflationary trend, or the United States Army field generals' reports in 1965 and 1966 of "*seeing* the light at the end of the tunnel" (in Vietnam). The optimistic person relies on the belief that he has considered the relevant factors from the long-term point of view. He has specific reasons for his optimism, which he believes he can share (with the same results) with all those who see clearly and take the long-range point of view.[17]

If someone else contests his optimism, the optimist may reconsider what is desirable, what the facts are, what the causal implications of the facts are likely to be, etc. Having taken the position of a spectator with particularly keen sight, the optimist is open to such challenges. He can and will change his mind if any challenge makes its mark tellingly.

The person who HOPES is involved personally, much like the person who loves another. Being thus involved, the one who HOPES does not see his situation merely from an objective viewpoint. For example, an illness in which one is personally involved is not seen as hardly more than the breakdown of an apparatus. However, the objective viewpoint may be quite appropriate for the doctor who, with a clear head, must diagnose and attempt to cure the ailment. As a result of his examination, the doctor may be optimistic about his patient's recovery. But unless he becomes personally involved, he will not HOPE that the person will recover.

Let us return to the examples cited earlier. In each case, the personal involvement was crucial. (i) I am ill and hope to recover. I feel that to fail to hope would be to betray myself; I should lose my integrity. (ii) A loved one is seriously ill. I hope for his recovery. I feel that, despite the odds, not to hope for his recovery would be to deny our relationship; but that relationship is "too real," "too much a part of me," to be denied. (iii) Being imprisoned and realizing that there is a chance for deliverance, not to rely on it is to give myself up as lost too soon. Hence, I feel that either I must hope for deliverance or lose my self-respect and integrity. (iv) Not to hope for reunion with my family—now separated from them by war—is to cut myself off from them. It is to deny my membership; in effect, to be disloyal to them. (v) My country is occupied by enemy troops. I hope for deliverance. I feel that to have any other reaction in these circumstances would be to react treasonably. In short, in all these cases—because of some personal involvement—not to hope is seen as betrayal or treason. Thus, despair is seen as a *temptation*, an alluring possibility that must be resisted. Loyalty demands hope.

The view of reality operative in the person who HOPES need not contradict that of the spectator. It may qualify it. The sense of integrity, the sense of commitment to another, etc., are taken by the one who HOPES to be integral aspects of the situation. For instance, (iv) (hoping to be reunited with one's family), it is assumed that one's actions need not, and need not be thought to, effect an actual reunion; nevertheless, the one who hopes construes not hoping as a betrayal, because *not hoping* for reunion is incompatible with his love of his family. Usually, as in (i), (iii), and (v), one who hopes construes his personal response as bearing directly on his objective without actually effecting it. Hence, not to hope is treason or betrayal. Not to hope is to renege on a commitment; it is to fail to keep one's part of the bargain. In a word it is to be disloyal.

The state of mind of the person who hopes, as in cases (i) and (v), is somewhat parallel to the state of mind of any good athlete before participating in a game. He has resolved that his team will win, and he will do his utmost to succeed. He is quietly confident that his team will win, even if the odds-makers have determined that the opposing team is strongly favored.[18]

Since HOPE is based on these wider personal and relational characteristics, a determination of its probability—based simply on objectively determined (intersubjectively verifiable) cause-effect estimates—is not crucial. Probability calculations are seen by the person who HOPES as superficial considerations, for they neglect the most essential features of the situation.

Marcel says:

> It [HOPE] implies a kind of radical refusal to reckon possibilities, and this is enormously important. It is as though it carried with it as postulate the assertion that reality overflows all possible reckonings; as though it claimed, in virtue of some unknown secret affinity, to touch a principle hidden in the heart of things, or rather in the heart of events, which mocks such reckonings.[19]

Marcel rather over-states the case. One who hopes is not obliged to hold the radical view regarding reasoning about outcomes that he advances. I should like to offer a more reasonable and less radical interpretation that is still consistent with Marcel's general position. It is not that the person who HOPES closes himself off from the probable facts of the case. To HOPE need not be positively irrational. The position of the person who HOPES is rather that there are additional considerations which he must attend to—the personal and relational factors discussed above—which are not called into play in determining what the probable facts are. And these are such that, *in principle*, they cannot be made part of the calculations. Consider another analogy. To HOPE that some event will occur or some proposition is true is to have a stance in relation to that event or proposition parallel to that of the would-be discoverer or inventor, not (as with optimism) parallel to that of the technician. The technician has no objective unless he sees approximately how to achieve it. He has a rather firm basis from which he works and makes calculations pointing to his end or goal. The inventor or discoverer inevitably has much less to go on than the technician. He has no proven formulas or maps with which to make calculations concerning the likelihood or location of his goal. Yet he sets out resolving that, if the goal is attainable, he will attain it. The person who HOPES similarly resolves that, if the desired possibility is attainable, it will be attained. And that resolve does not logically depend on the calculated odds of seeing one's way through to success.

Perhaps an earlier remark, that the experience of HOPE is less likely to be widespread in a technological society such as ours is somewhat clearer now. We are conditioned in a technological society to wait for evidence, to proceed only after the computer has flashed the green light.

In the last chapter, we observed that J. P. Day construes the estimation of probabilities as a necessary condition of hope. In effect, Day conceives hope more in accord with the technician's than the discoverer's attitude. Marcel, on the other hand seems to hold that calculation cannot even accompany hope. And I have argued that, although calculation is not an essential feature of hope, it is not incompatible with it either. The calculation of probabilities can accompany hope even in the special cases being examined as long as undue importance is not placed on it. Still, Marcel is right—as against Day: one often hopes even when one refuses or is unable to calculate probabilities (say, because of one's position relative to the evidence) or when one knows that a particular calculation yields negative results. In our terminology, only optimism bears the relation to the calculation of probabilities that Day claims to obtain among all cases of hope. As we have seen, however, the connection is not required for the range of hope specifically under discussion here.

To use Søren Kierkegaard's phrase, hope, is "the passion for the possible." HOPE does not wait for probability calculations. HOPE risks and ventures (as did Abraham, according to the biblical account) without the security of maps and a well-trod path. Outcomes are not guaranteed, and success need be neither likely nor expected. He who HOPES simply presses on, refusing to give up or to close the door on the possibility of that for which he hopes. Marcel says that the experience of HOPING for something is analogous to that of advancing credit. Both involve a commitment, which in turn involves a risk. Optimism (as the term is here used) takes less of a risk or takes a risk of a different kind, for it relies on favorable probabilities before making a commitment. One who HOPES finds himself committed independently of such probability estimates. What is HOPED for may not occur and it may not even be probable. Everything is staked on the possibility that it will occur. Conversely, much can be lost: ". . . there is always the danger that hope will meet with the direst disappointment. . . ."[20] The person who hopes runs the clear risk of finding himself in a situation in which he is "a creditor facing an insolvent debtor."[21]

Let us consider more carefully, therefore, what happens, phenomenologically, to a person whose hopes are thus disappointed. Suppose someone dies, someone who has been seriously ill and whose recovery I have hoped for. If I had made my own self-fulfillment depend on the continuing life of the deceased, I could easily have fallen into debilitating despair. If, however, I maintained my independence and sense of identity appropriately during my commitment to the one who has just died, I need not collapse on his death. Still I will feel rather like a creditor facing an insolvent debtor. I committed myself, my time, my love, my energy to this person and to his recovery. I lost. Yet, I am comforted in knowing that, by hoping, I have remained steadfast in my love. If it is essential to my concept of my *self* to be committed as a loving person (to be committed to persons like the deceased), then I have succeeded in an essential project. I am what I desire to be. Had I not taken the risk of hope (though I lost), I should feel that I was untrue to my intended commitment. As Antoine says in Marcel's play, *Le Mort de Demain*: "To love somebody is to say to him, 'You will not die.'" I made the same affirmation as long as it was possible. Hence, I stood the test; I remained firm in my love even when it made me vulnerable. Disappointment, however painful, need not be self-destructive. There is no need to feel that it would have been better not to have hoped at all. The disappointment was worth the effort, for, in risking myself thus, I have upheld one of my most central commitments concerning my relation to others.

Disappointment of hopes tends to be self-destructive only if one has placed certain extreme requirements either on one's hopes for oneself or on what is possible. Imagine I am an invalid and have set a specific time (say, Christmas) by which I must be cured, i.e., walk again. The time comes but I am not cured. (i) One possibility is that I will despair. I will give up. Of course, this option presupposes that I have linked the cure—walking again—with self-fulfillment. I am implicitly saying, "unless I am cured I am doomed." A counselor would normally try to direct the invalid away from such an association. Surely, the hope of walking again cannot rest solely on walking by a certain date. (ii) Another possibility is that I will extend the time limit (for example, to Easter). This may avoid the disappointment or simply postpone it. It does not, however, get to the heart of the difficulty. (iii) Or, I might come to believe that everything would not be lost even if there were no cure. Such a realization could support a genuine solution; if I held the belief emotionally as well as cognitively, my attitude toward recovery or non-recovery would be radically different from that of possibility (i). My invalid status would no longer constitute a threat to my selfhood. Still, there are rather different ways in which I could hold this belief about myself and my possibilities. Option (iii) might appear as (iiia): despairing that I will be cured but not despairing of myself. This alternative is, in effect, a version of Stoicism; one adopts a resigned acceptance of one's plight. Option (iii) might appear as (iiib): hoping that I will be cured but not linking or identifying the cure with self-fulfillment. (iiia) avoids self-destructive disappointment by abandoning certain desires. One cannot be disappointed if one has no hopes or expectations that can be dashed. (iiib) avoids self-destructive disappointment by refusing to restrict the relevance of what is possible and by refusing to equate self-fulfillment with any perceived range of possibilities.

Whereas disappointment is the non-fulfillment of hopes, despair is the *anticipation* of non-fulfillment. Where one has made his self-fulfillment depend entirely on the continued life of someone who subsequently dies, one has utterly given up all possibility of his own continued or further development. He cannot but anticipate that all his hopes will remain unfulfilled. By that death, the door to his own future has been closed. He sees no possible way of going on with the life he wants, or of escaping his sorrow and his sense of being lost and alone. He is in despair.

Jean-Paul Sartre's *No Exit* expresses very clearly the sense that, in deep despair, one sees no way of moving into the future, not even the future of one's own self-destruction. In *Sickness Unto Death*, Søren Kierkegaard similarly describes deep despair as the feeling that, although one is in an intolerable situation, all doors—even the doors of death—have been closed:

> . . . The torment of despair is precisely this, not to be able to die. So it has much in common with the situation of the moribund when he lies and struggles with death, and cannot die. So to be sick unto death is, not to be able to die—yet not as though there were hope of life; no, the hopelessness in this case is that even the last hope, death, is not available. When death is the greatest danger, one hopes for life; but when one becomes acquainted with an even more dreadful danger, one hopes for death. So when the danger is so great that death has become one's hope, despair is the disconsolateness of not being able to die. [22]

In this extreme despair, as Paul Tillich remarks, "one has come to the end of his possibilities." He sees his future as closed; the anticipated future offers no possibility of genuine fulfillment.

A religion of hope, like Marcel's, advocates that one must avoid limits and qualifications both regarding one's hopes for oneself and regarding what is relevantly possible. No restrictive conditions are to be placed on the possibilities for one's self-fulfillment. In this sense, Marcel adopts alternative (iiib). Refusing to limit the possible, Marcel actually holds that ultimate personal fullfillment may take place beyond the finite realm of this life. Some may criticize such a religion from the perspective of (iiia), for they deny the legitimacy of reaching beyond the finite. They hold that we must disclaim such aspirations.

This sort of criticism is often made by anti-religious writers against all religious (or theistic) views. But it is actually more suitably applied to certain forms of religion than to others. I hold that it is not successful against a religion based on hope—which will be shortly outlined. It does, however, have some force when leveled against a religion of optimism.

One salient difference between a religion of optimism and a religion of HOPE is epistemological. Those taking the alternative of optimism are convinced that an objective view of the evidence will yield the desired theistic conclusion. Those who take the alternative of HOPE are not convinced that such a conclusion follows on objective grounds. Another important difference is psychological. Those who HOPE stress the importance of risk, passionate commitment, a sense of loyalty and morality, venture, and the uncertainty of a religious stance. Those who take the optimistic alternative will not regard all of these features as essential. Characteristically, they downplay the element of venture and deny that the uncertainty is irretrievable. (We shall return to examine these differences in some detail in the following chapters.)

Conclusion

Our phenomenological examination of HOPE may be focused by a final look at our examples. Speaking metaphorically, to hope for something is to be disposed to do what one can to keep the door to it unlocked. Consider the invalid case: As an invalid, I will be disposed to act in whatever way I believe may aid in my recovery. If I think that moving around in a wheelchair will serve, I will be so disposed to act. If I do not think it helpful, I will not be so disposed. If I hope for deliverance (as distinct from escape) from a concentration camp, I will be inclined to do what I believe will keep me alive until the day of deliverance. I will be disposed to avoid danger whenever possible. I will probably be disposed to encourage others. I will probably be disposed to listen to reports of the activities of Allied forces. I will probably be disposed to imagine what I will be doing after I'm out, etc. If I am separated from my wife—say that I am a German in World War II and my wife, a prisoner in Russia—now that the war is over, I shall hope to be reunited with her. There may be nothing I can actually do to bring about her return or to effect our reunion. But I will be disposed to refrain from having her declared legally dead or having my marriage annulled. I will be disposed to keep my life open in this respect.

We may combine the results of Chapters I and II in a formula thus: A person HOPES that p (where p is a substitute for any proposition or event hoped for) = keeping his life open or fluid with respect to p—where (a) neither p nor not-p is certain for him, (b) he wants p and (c) he sees p as constructively connected with his own well-being and/or concept of himself as a person.

In the following chapters, we shall consider whether religious experience may be restructured, or seen as a hoping of the profound sort here examined. In order to keep our task manageable, I shall confine discussion to Christian experience and theology. But we must ask, first, whether such hopes can be justified in the face of objections reasonably posed against cherishing just such hopes.

3 Believing and Hoping

Let us, in order to apply what we have learned about the structure and phenomenology of hope to the issues of the philosophy of religion, begin by contrasting hoping and believing.

A Comparison of Believing and Hoping

In our formula "*S* (a person) hopes that *p* (a proposition or event)," hope takes a subject and an object. Similarly, in the standard formula "*S* believes that *p*," belief takes a subject and object. We had asked, earlier, what logical conditions must obtain in order that *p* might serve as an object of hope for *S*? A parallel question may be posed for belief: What logical conditions must obtain in order that *p* might serve as an object of belief for *S*?

Clearly, the necessary conditions for an object of hope are not the necessary conditions for an object of belief. This can be readily demonstrated. A person, *S*, may believe that *p* and yet not want or desire that *p*. Wanting and believing are logically *independent*. To put the point another way, believing that *p* is non-evaluative of *p*, whereas hoping that *p* necessarily is evaluative of *p*. Furthermore, a difference arises regarding modal elements. In cases of hope, we hold that "neither *p* nor not-*p* is certain for *S*" or that "*S* takes *p* to be possible." But *S* cannot be said to believe that *p* (where *p* concerns the future), if *S* does not actually *expect* that *p*, if S thinks that p is merely possible. By contrast S can hope that p when S believes p merely to be possible. Again S may believe that p when p is certain for S. Belief is logically compatible with certainty.[1] But, of course, S could not (merely) hope that p if p were certain.

Although it would be beyond the scope of this essay to go into a detailed discussion of the truth-conditions of belief-ascriptions, as has been done with hope-ascriptions, it is to the point to suggest some of the conditions that must obtain in order that p be the object of S's belief. For purposes of this essay, the notion "S believes that p" may be left relatively unanalysed. In fact, if A. Phillips Griffiths is right (I am inclined to agree with him), the notion *must* remain unanalysed—i.e., "belief" is actually not reducible to more simple concepts.[2]

Perhaps p must be considered by S to be probable, in order to qualify as S's belief. (The sense of "probable" intended is that in which p is said to be probable only if the odds that p are 50 percent or better.) This proposal may be challenged by the following counterexample. A gambler is said to *believe* that p (p = "I will win the next game") in spite of the fact that p is not probable. He also believes that the chances that p are one out of ten (ten percent). (It is irrelevant, here, that the gambler's belief is either irrational or unjustified.) If this be granted, then it will not do to say that a necessary condition for S's believing that p is that S consider p to be probable (in the sense defined). What then, *in this case*, does it mean to say that the gambler believes that he will win? In part, it means that he *expects* to win. That is, he anticipates a certain outcome. His expectation is exhibited by the fact that he is prepared to bet. On the other hand, if, given normal gambling conditions, etc.,[3] he is unwilling to place a bet on p, we are likely to say that S does not really believe that p. The gambler himself might concede, "I thought I believed I would win the next game, but now that the chips are down I see that I don't."

Hence unwillingness on S's part to perform certain actions relative to p is strong evidence that S does not believe that p.

However, the mere fact that our gambler is prepared to bet hardly entails that he believes that *p*. He might be prepared to bet, for example, if he (strongly) *hopes* that *p*. As was earlier argued, if *S* hopes that *p* it does not follow that *S* expects that *p*—he merely believes that *p* is possible, wants *p*, etc. *S*'s hope that *p* may, then, be sufficient grounds for *S* to bet that *p*. (Of course, *S* may hope that *p* and, given other considerations, never bet that *p*.) Behavior, therefore, may not distinguish satisfactorily between hoping and believing that *p*. And yet, they are obviously not the same.

If *S* believes that *p* but (apart from his bet) does not care whether *p* obtains or not, what *S* will bet depends on *the degree of his confidence* that *p* as well as his means, his interests, etc. If, however, *S* hopes that *p* but does not believe that *p*, what *S* will bet depends on the *strength of his desire* that *p*, as well as his means, etc. But his interest is already engaged. So although hope and belief are quite different, the same behavior may be motivated by either.

Suppose that *S* (who believed that *p*) loses his bet and knows it. That is, *S* discovers that not-*p*. No doubt, *S* would be *surprised*. Whether he is mildly surprised, shocked, or in some intermediate state of mind will doubtless depend on the strength of his former confidence that *p*. But suppose instead that *S*, hoping that *p*, discovers that he has lost his bet. No doubt, *S* would be *disappointed*. Whether he is mildly or profoundly disappointed, or is in some intermediate state of mind, will depend primarily on the strength of his desire that *p*. Of course, his earlier assessment of the evidence may make the disappointment more profound and unsettling, for it may have led him to expect a favorable outcome. But that is a mere complication. Surprise and disappointment remain two entirely different mental states, in spite of the fact that they may be manifested in the same behavior.

Let us consider another example in which certain dispositions to behavior will be the same whether one hopes or believes that *p*. Suppose that *S*, a husband returning from the Viet Nam conflict, is confronted with evidence that his wife has been unfaithful. In spite of the evidence, *S* believes that p (p = "my wife has been faithful"). Suppose, also, that the equally unfortunate P, S's buddy in Viet Nam, is confronted with evidence that *his* wife has been unfaithful. In spite of the evidence, given his loyalty to his wife, P hopes that p. Neither S nor P will be disposed to file for divorce as a result of being confronted with the evidence. Neither S nor P will be inclined to hire a private eye to trail his wife or search for "skeletons in the closet." Both S and P will probably be inclined to belittle the evidence, etc.

There are, of course, cases in which the dispositions to behavior will *not* be similar, depending on whether one hopes that p or believes that p. The reason has already been suggested. S's hope that p often entails that S is disposed to try to bring it about that p. However, S's belief that p does not (*qua* belief) ever entail that S is disposed to try to bring it about that p—for wanting and believing are logically independent. If I believe that a bloody civil war is very likely to engulf the United States, I will not *thereby* be disposed to try to bring it about or to try to stop it.

There is a closer, or simpler, relationship between hope and action than there is between belief and action. Hoping that p entails being disposed to perform actions that S believes to be conducive to bringing it about that p. (There may, of course, be overriding reasons for not performing such actions.) No such entailment, however, holds for beliefs. So, in order to specify particular behavioral dispositions as part of the notion of "S believes that p," one must assume particular hypothetical wants. For example, if S believes that it is raining outside, then, if S does not want to get wet and if . . . , then S will take his umbrella. In the cases of the gambler who believes he will win and the husband who believes his wife was faithful, actual *wants* or desires have already been built into the story. The gambler *qua* gambler wants to bet and win; the husband *qua* traditional husband wants a faithful wife.

Anyone who wishes to give a strict dispositional account of "S believes that p" will have difficulty, in some cases, distinguishing between believing and hoping. Alexander Bain, who defines belief dispositionally, construes hope merely as a special type of belief. "Hope," he says, "is the well-known name for belief in some contingent future bringing good."[4] But if the foregoing discussion is conceded, Bain must be mistaken in this claim: hope- and belief-ascriptions have different truth-conditions. The truth-conditions for ascribing hope are not merely a subset of the conditions for belief-ascriptions.

Returning to the case of the gambler, we may discern another difference between hoping and believing. Since the action in both cases is the same, namely, betting on p, one might be tempted to think that the same criticism holds, whether the action was motivated by believing that p or by hoping that p. Yet clearly one might approve of S's hoping that p while discounting S's believing that p. The difference in the grounds for hoping and believing might justify a difference in evaluation. Why is this so?

Clearly, the conservative principle that one ought not to bet on p unless the odds that p are reasonably good is decidedly prejudicial. We have observed several times that, although hoping that p entails thinking that p is possible, believing that p (for future events) entails expecting that p. In the gambler's case, betting is a *risk*. In fact, it is a considerable risk. The hopeful gambler is (or at least could be) aware of the risk involved in his action. Desiring that p, he is committed to no more than that p is possible. But the believing gambler cannot (in the face of the evidence) be fully aware of the risk. Expecting that p he must hide from himself the element of risk. Hence, we are inclined to explain his holding his belief in terms of self-deception. It is worth adding that, in general, people tend to deprecate rather strongly such self-deception. Although we may view the hopeful gambler as reckless rather than as courageous, we tend to reserve our harsher judgment for the believing gambler who bets in accord with poor odds. To return to an earlier metaphor, whereas when one hopes that p (without believing that p) one fixes on the possibility that the door to p will not be locked, when one believes that p one expects that the door is or will be open.

We have been comparing "S hopes that p" and "S believes that p." These expressions will now be compared with "S believes in p." Believing that p and believing in p are *not* synonymous in a wide range of cases. Admittedly, some uses of "S believes in p," may, without loss of meaning, be translated as "S believes that p exists." For example, if it is said that S believes in fairies or in the Loch Ness monster, very likely what is meant is no more than that S believes that fairies exist or that there is a Loch Ness monster. The more interesting cases of "believing in" are either not reducible to, or not so easily reducible to, cases of "believing that." For example:

(i)   "S believes in Santa Claus."
(ii) "S believes in his doctor."
(iii) "S believes in the United Nations."
(iv) "S believes in mandatory wage-price controls."

One obvious use of (i) is easily reducible to the belief that Santa Claus exists. But, clearly, there is another familiar use that is not thus reducible. A small child may no longer believe in Santa Claus because Santa Claus no longer brings her the sorts of gifts she likes. Although she does not doubt that Santa Claus exists, she no longer has confidence in him—she no longer believes *in* him.[5] Of course, (ii), (iii), and (iv) cannot, on any reasonable analysis, reduce to belief, respectively, that the doctor, the United Nations, mandatory wage-price controls exist. An analysis of (iv) in terms of "belief that" need not even include the thesis that mandatory controls actually exist. So belief *in* p cannot, in some cases, reduce to belief *that* p and, in other cases, does not actually entail the belief that p.

We speak of belief in God and belief in life after death as well as belief that God exists and belief that there is a life after death. Whether these beliefs-in ought to be analyzed in accord with (i), (ii) and (iv) will be discussed in Chapter V. For the moment, we need keep in mind only that the linguistic distinction between "belief that" and "belief in" may reflect a deeper philosophical distinction. Anticipating a major part of our argument, namely, that religious-belief can best be understood as a close analogue of HOPE, we shall later attempt to show that the beliefs *that* God exists and *that* there is life after death are not proper parts of the analysis of "belief in God" and "belief in life after death"—just as belief that there are mandatory wage-price controls would not normally be part of the analysis of (iv). Instead, we shall suggest an analysis in terms of the beliefs that "possibly, God exists" and "possibly, there is life after death."

"Beliefs in" (in the non-reducible sense) have a *prospective* character that is not a feature of "beliefs that." When, for example, one believes in his doctor, he not only believes that his doctor is and has been professionally able; he also trusts or has confidence that his doctor will continue thus. In this sense, "believes in" is similar to "hopes that." Both have a similar evaluative element (e.g., one who believes *in* his doctor judges that it is a *good* thing that he is good at his profession). Here, we note only a few of the interesting parallels between "S believes in p" and "S hopes that p"—which, later, will provide the foundation on which the analysis of religious-belief as HOPE will be developed.

A Comparison of Justified Belief and Justified Hope

Many philosophers have been concerned with what is required in order to justify a person's *belief* that p. John Locke, for example, suggests a common sense view of the justification of belief, which we may render thus: "S is justified in believing that p" if and only if "S's assent to p is equal to the evidence that p, and p coheres with S's other beliefs." By "evidence" is meant phenomena generally accepted as evidence[6] which a person in S's situation could reasonably be expected to have.[7] On Locke's view, one's assent—the strength of one's belief—must follow the strength of his evidence. One's belief that p depends on the evidence for p.

On this Lockean criterion, both criticism and support of non-evaluative, factual beliefs are justifiably tendered: (a) on evidential grounds; and (b) on grounds of coherence with other beliefs already held. It is beyond the scope of this essay to argue for any particular criterion of justified belief. But since this criterion is rather widely accepted and enjoys a measure of initial plausibility, I shall simply adopt it as a model for the purpose of developing a criterion of justified hope. Later, we shall examine it a little more critically.

A formal notion of justified hope probably does not take a clear form in ordinary discourse. Still, we do see fit to criticize, or object to, a person's holding certain hopes. We often regard a person's hopes as moral or immoral; and we often charge that they are foolish or silly or unwarranted. In this essay, I want to use the notion of justified hope as an umbrella term. If a hope is justified, it is unobjectionable. If it can meet provisional objections appropriately brought against it, it is—according to the present use of the expression —a justified and/or justifiable hope.

Comparison of the following sentence-pairs helps to bring out a crucial difference between evaluating belief-statements and evaluating hope-statements. Suppose you were to hear the following utterances in ordinary discourse. What responses are likely to be forthcoming?

1. I believe that the President will be assassinated when he comes to the campus to defend his policies.
2. I hope that the President will be assassinated when he comes to the campus to defend his policies.
3. I believe that if you step out of the door, you will be killed.
4. I hope that if you step out of the door, you will be killed.
5. I believe that the souls of non-believers suffer eternal damnation in hell.

6.   I hope that the souls of non-believers suffer eternal damnation in hell.

One's reaction to the odd-numbered belief-statements is bound to be quite different from that to the even-numbered hope-statements. With regard to the former, one wants to know what evidence the speaker has to back his claim up. "Have you heard any threats on the President's life?" "Is a radical group conspiring to kill the President?" "Has a saboteur infiltrated the secret service?" With regard to the latter, one is likely to respond by asking what (moral) right the speaker has for hoping or wanting such a thing. "No matter how much you disagree with the President's policy, it's wrong to hope that he will be assassinated. His policy should be defeated by the ballot, not the bullet."

To hope that p, where p is a non-evaluative proposition (e.g., "The President will be assassinated when he comes to the campus") is to place an evaluation on p. But to believe that p does not entail such an evaluation. For belief-statements, commitment to p is a function of the evidence for p. This is emphatically not true of hope-statements. If S hopes that p, S's hope is subject to moral appraisal because desire (an element of hope) is subject to moral scrutiny. So a necessary consideration in determining whether S's hope that p is justified is whether it is morally acceptable. But even when hope-statements meet the moral criterion, we do not insist that commitment to the object of hope be equal to the evidence for it. Consider the following sentence-pairs:

7.   I believe their ship is seaworthy, although much of the evidence seems to point in the other direction.
8.   I hope their ship is seaworthy, although much of the evidence seems to point in the other direction.
9.   I believe my daughter will recover, despite the fact that nearly all the evidence is negative.
10.   I hope my daughter will recover, despite the fact that nearly all the evidence is negative.
11.   I believe my husband (who was taken prisoner) will return: yet, given the conditions of war, I see no way

of getting any positive evidence for it.

12. I hope my husband (who was taken prisoner) will return; yet, given the conditions of war, I see no way of getting any positive evidence for it.

These belief-statements violate the Lockean criterion of justified belief. In each case, assent to p is greater than the evidence for p. If it seems reasonable to require that the strength of beliefs be proportional to the strength of evidence, any comparable constraint on hopes seems much too restrictive.

Even the most rigorous Lockean would not wish to place such severe strictures on hope. Hopes are already constrained by the moral condition, but beliefs are not. We simply make hopes and beliefs responsible in different ways. Moral (but non-evidential) appraisal correctly roots out irresponsible hopes, but not (non-evaluative) beliefs. On the other hand, an evidential requirement is the one and only means to insure responsible belief (though this is sometimes expressed in terms of a moral right to believe). Since the entire case for responsible belief must rest on the evidential requirement, there is good reason for maintaining a strict standard. Yet, consistent with a strict standard for belief, it seems reasonable to concede a permissive *evidential requirement* for hope.

In addition to moral scrutiny, hopes must meet a *pragmatic test*. A hope is not justified or justifiable if it is judged correctly to be foolish or silly or not in S's best interest. As we have seen, one does not hope for what he does not prefer on balance. As observers, however, it may be clear to us that S's desire for p may not be compatible with most of his other desires, that S's priorities are mixed up, or that he ought (pragmatically) to prefer another alternative. We may be able to demonstrate that his life would be better if he reordered his pursuits, including p. For example, we may judge that it is foolish (even if the evidence were somewhat favorable) for a particular young woman to hope any longer for the return of her boyfriend missing in action for five years—assuming her other desires and aspirations. We may feel that we can show that she has not correctly ordered her priorities or correctly weighted conflicting desires.

We have observed that the evidential requirement for justifiable hope is considerably weaker than it is for justifiable belief. The most that could be required seems to be that one be able to demonstrate that there are good grounds for affirming the real *possibility* of the object of hope. In hoping that p, the one who hopes must *believe* that p is actually possible. On the Lockean criterion, that belief must be supported by adequate evidence. Ought more to be required? Are there good reasons for making the evidential criterion for justifiable hope less permissive?

Of course, in cases where one hopes and also believes that p, the evidential requirement must be stronger; it must include the requirement for justifiable belief. However, where one merely hopes that p, there is no compelling reason to strengthen the requirement. Only the actual possibility of p seems needed. If there is positive evidence for p, so much the better. It may, in fact, be needed to justify one's *strongly* hoping for p.

In general, if a hope is to be justified, any belief that it presupposes must meet the conditions for justified belief— e.g., beliefs about what is possible, expected outcomes, strength of evidence, etc. Determining whether such supporting beliefs—the context in which the hope is embedded—are justified, I will call the *background beliefs test*. Assuming that one's hope can meet the four tests—the moral, pragmatic, real possibility, and background beliefs tests—the strength of S's desire that p and the strength of the evidence that p combine to determine the appropriate strength of S's hope that p. It may be appropriate to hope strongly for p even when the evidence for p is quite weak, if the desire for p is considerable. For example, assuming a parent's natural desire, one may be justified in strongly hoping for the recovery of one's young daughter even though the doctor's prognosis does not offer very good odds. An Israeli woman, whose husband has been taken prisoner on the Syrian front, may, given the politics of war, have no way of determining whether he is alive or dead or whether he will ever return. Yet because of her love, because of her desire to be reunited, because of her commitment to him, we would probably agree that she was justified in strongly hoping th..: he :·ill return—i.e., justified in living in such a way as to keep the door open to this desired possibility. We might even feel, given the strength of her desire and the moral commitment involved, that it would be positively wrong or inappropriate for her to give up hope.

In summary, if I say that someone's hope is not justified, then I must be prepared to affirm that his hope does not pass the four-fold test outlined above. The appropriate strength of a hope that satisfies that test is, in effect, the sum of the strengths of the desire and of the supporting evidence.

Assessment of the Criteria of Justified Belief and Justified Hope

We had, for ease of comparison, availed ourselves of Locke's common sense criterion. But our argument did not actually depend on accepting as austere a criterion as that. In fact (as will be seen), Locke's constraint is somewhat too restrictive. Its initial plausibility and wide acceptance made it a reasonable point of departure. However, without damaging our own argument, we can if needed, modify the criterion of justified belief. One of the advantages of the Lockean notion is that it can be used to oppose dogmatism and fanaticism. It requires that adherence to all propositions depends on having sufficient evidential support. If one can be justified only thus, then, clearly, dogmatic views may be discounted at once.

We expect fair-minded people to apportion their assent to particular propositions on the strength of the relevant evidence. For example, when a presiding judge instructs a juror as to how to consider the evidence presented, the juror is implicitly being asked to follow as closely as possible the maxim of proportioning assent to strength of evidence relative to reaching a verdict. Often, even if one is unwilling to adhere to the requirement in one's own case, we are quick to regard it as a fault in another—particularly where we do not share the belief in question. Nevertheless, strict adherence to the Lockean criterion does not seem to be altogether required. Some examples will make this clear.

However, before considering the limitations of the Lockean criterion, we should perhaps note other familiar cases in which beliefs thought to be justified in spite of their failure to satisfy the Lockean criterion are actually not so obviously justified. Consider the classic case of the supposed duty of Victorian ladies to believe their husbands to be faithful, or the case of the supposed duty of a mother to believe her son to be innocent of a crime. If we supposed that people had a moral duty to believe such propositions (e.g., "My husband is faithful," "My son is innocent") in the face of the evidence to the contrary, it would follow that there were cases in which one would not be obliged to apportion assent to evidence. (Indeed, one would be obliged *not* to apportion assent to evidence.)

Let us look at one of these cases more closely. Suppose one's son is innocent and yet thought by the press and public (for some reason) to have been involved in a horrible crime. It may well comfort the son that his mother believes him to be innocent. Loyalty and the parental bond may invite her belief. But the case for a *duty to believe* him to be innocent is obviously more difficult to defend than the case for a *duty to hope* he is innocent. Not to have hoped for his innocence would have betrayed their relationship.

The reasoning here is similar to that involved in the earlier examples of hope. *S* hopes that his friend, who is seriously ill, will recover, and he feels that not to hope would be a betrayal of their friendship. Separated from his family, *S* hopes to be reunited, and he feels that not to hope would be a denial of family membership. *S* hopes that his country will not be defeated, and feels that not to hope would be treasonable.

In the case of the suspicious spouse, not to hope that her husband had been faithful would be a denial of loyalty, for it would imply that the wife did not particularly want the marriage vows to be intact (or care whether they were intact). It is the appropriateness of the desire that her husband be faithful that seems to be the basis for the supposed obligation. Without in any way shaking her desire that he be faithful, the wife may of course, have doubts about her husband's actual faithfulness. So, if the moral obligation arises from the fact that she should desire that her husband be faithful, then it does not follow that *belief* in her husband's faithfulness is obligatory. What follows, given the possibility of his faithfulness, is that hope is a duty. Perhaps, then, the intuition behind the supposed duty to believe even against the evidence can be fully explained by a duty to hope (though not to believe) against the evidence.

In some situations in which one holds that a wife does have a duty to believe her husband innocent even when others have good reason to doubt his faithfulness, the spouse may have evidence of character and intent (drawn from the marriage relationship) not available to most other people. In such cases, the spouse need not believe against the evidence; she may also have well-founded beliefs about her husband with which the belief that he has been unfaithful does not cohere. For others, however, the belief that he has been unfaithful may fit quite easily and coherently with the majority of the rest of their beliefs. In short, there is normally no reason to hold that if a wife has a duty to believe her husband innocent (on the basis of privileged evidence), her duty requires violating the strong criterion for justified belief.

If we have a case in which there is no dispute or question about the evidence and the strength of the evidence, if all parties agree (the wife and others) that the evidence of the husband's infidelity is quite strong, or (the mother and others) that the evidence of the son's guilt is quite strong, then it seems unlikely that we would say that the wife (or mother) had a *duty to believe* the husband (or son) innocent. We might, in such circumstances, wish to say that the wife (or mother) had a *right to believe* her husband (or son) innocent. That is, given the account of belief offered earlier, the wife may be said to have a right to feel secure in her husband's affections, and the mother, a right to feel secure in her son's good name. Admitting such an epistemic right requires going beyond the Lockean standard of justified belief. It does seem reasonable however, to maintain that, in just these sorts of cases involving both belief and HOPE, Locke's criterion of justified belief is simply too stringent.

Another range of beliefs for which philosophers, for instance William James[8], have argued that the Lockean criterion is too restrictive are those that tend to verify themselves. For example, sometimes, if, despite evidence to the contrary, a mother persists in her belief that her child is well-behaved, it is quite likely that the child will become well-behaved. If a person always thinks well of others and believes that they will respond positively to him, it is likely that his beliefs will become confirmed in a significant range of cases—even though his initial beliefs were clearly false and contrary to the evidence. The reason is simply that people often respond to the beliefs others hold about them. As psychologists never tire of telling us, when parents and teachers drum into a child the idea that he is stupid, he may easily become dull and uninterested in learning even if he was not so originally. As James points out, if (among the beliefs in question) belief that p is a necessary condition for the occurrence of p then although the evidence may be against p, it would be unreasonable or imprudent to adhere slavishly to the maxim that assent must be equal to the evidence. Such a policy would obviously deprive us of an important benefit.

Still, the question arises as to whether belief that p is actually a necessary condition for p (even if it were a sufficient condition). Might not the same results obtain if one strongly desired them, thought them possible, and assiduously *hoped* they would be actualized? But if hoping that p were sufficient to produce the desired results (and I think they sometimes are), then since hoping would not require assent to a proposition to which there was insufficient evidence, one need hardly conclude that beliefs that tend to verify themselves require a relaxation of the standard that, in believing that p, assent must be equal to evidence. It may then seem entirely reasonable to concede that it *is* much too restrictive to disallow beliefs that tend to verify themselves, if they succeed at last in passing the sort of moral and pragmatic tests which must be met by justified hopes.

All in all, the Lockean criterion appears to be too restrictive to be thought to apply to all cases of belief. In particular, in cases in which one's belief is also one's hope, and one's hope meets the requirements for justified hopes, there are good reasons for holding that the beliefs themselves are justified in spite of the fact that they are not strictly apportioned to the evidence. If so, then justified hope sometimes allows one to go beyond the Lockean criterion: justified hopes sometimes justify freer or more generous beliefs relative to the evidence. That is, believing beyond the evidence may be permitted when the proposition in question has met at least the standards of justifiable hope—the moral, pragmatic, possibility and background beliefs tests discussed earlier.

The Lockean criterion of justified belief is usually appealed to (or merely assumed to obtain) by critics of religion, "faith-vetoers," and those who insist that intellectual integrity requires rejecting traditional religious outlooks. The traditional Western apologist may be tempted to defend his position by challenging the Lockean criterion, but that strategy seems to me to hold little promise. Although it may, as we have seen, be too restrictive and need to be replaced by a somewhat more permissive criterion, the required modifications would not be sufficient for the apologist's needs. Much more would be needed in order to justify, *as a system of beliefs*, the central tenets of traditional faith.

Our strategy is rather to meet the critic of religion on his own terms. Hence, I concede that any proposition *believed* (in the sense in which that is being used here) must meet the Lockean test. However, I mean to argue—what may seem initially implausible—that religious commitment, or faith, need not necessarily commit one to believing certain allegedly basic doctrines (e.g., "God exists," "There is a life after death"). Religious commitment is more similar, in the relevant respects, to HOPE than to ordinary belief. For example, in hoping that my daughter will recover, I am committed to the possibility that she will recover. I live in such a way as to keep the door open to that possibility; I am disposed to act in certain ways; etc. Nevertheless, I may not actually believe the proposition, "My daughter will recover." (Of course, neither do I believe, "My daughter will not recover." I believe that it is possible that she will recover.) So, too, one who adopts certain doctrines to guide his life (e.g., "There is life after death") need not thereby believe that the doctrine is true. (This is not to say that he believes it to be false. He takes it to be possible, morally and pragmatically desirable, etc.)

Because religious people are often called believers and because we speak of religious beliefs, we are inclined to accept rather uncritically the idea that religious commitment *entails* a belief that the objects of that commitment exist, or have existed, or will exist, etc. But, as we shall argue later, no such entailment actually obtains (even if those who are religious often do in fact believe that what they are committed to exist, have existed, or will come to pass, etc.). To view religious commitment as HOPE rather than as belief (that is, to view religious commitment as having HOPE as its closest analogue) serves, I wish to argue, not only as an effective answer to the critics of religion, but also as a model for a better understanding of the conceptual foundations of religion itself.

The task of the remaining chapters of this work, then, is two-fold. First, I intend to prove that some of the fundamental tenets of the major Western theistic religions pass the test for justifiable hope even if—as has been widely maintained by philosophers and others, particularly by those who follow Kant and Mill—they fail the justifiable beliefs test. For, if these tenets are held as hopes rather than as beliefs, a major intellectual and epistemological problem will have been solved at a stroke. I shall argue, that, therefore, concerning the objects of religious commitment, hope without belief is quite sufficient. Once it is established that these fundamental tenets are justifiable as hopes, I shall argue that other consid-

erations show that such an interpretation does not impover-
ish the religious tradition.

Conclusion

Let us, concluding this chapter, picture in rather straightforward terms the position of the theologian of hope. He
concedes, or insists, with the many critics of theology, that,
objectively speaking, the evidence for theism is at least
counterbalanced by the evidence against theism.[9] For example, the evidence of design alleged to prove God's existence,
the fact that men have a moral capacity, the fact that they
have religious experiences best described as experiences of
"seeing God," etc., is at least neutralized by the existence of
natural calamities (earthquakes, floods, and untimely deaths),
and moral atrocities (the Crusades, the Inquisition, the Nazi
ovens, and the My Lai massacre). Admitting this much, the
theologian of hope concedes that it is not possible to justify
the belief that God exists. But he perceives that many people
respond with hope to the tragic situation in which man
finds himself. He asks: (1) whether the theistic response of
hope can be justified, that is, whether it can meet the sorts of
objections appropriately raised against such a hope; and (2)
whether the response of hope, in the face of tragedy and
death, is an adequate foundation for religious commitments
of the Judeo-Christian sort.

The next chapter will deal with (1). The following two
chapters will deal with (2).

4 The Leap Toward the Transcendent

As was noted at the outset, both Kant and Mill held that the arguments and evidence for and against God's existence and for and against such things as life after death were indecisive. I am inclined to agree with their reasoning. Whether their assessment was correct or not is too large and distinct a topic to pursue fruitfully in this essay. It does, however, afford a reasonable assumption on which to proceed with the issues at hand. If, in addition, the religious commitment ought not to be denied to fully rational persons, then—rather as Kant and Mill felt (and as indeed I feel)—religion ought to be located in the realm of hope instead of the realm of belief. Such an adjustment provides a standard of justification more amenable to reason.

The groundwork for the hope alternative has now been completed (cf. the logical analysis of "hope," the phenomenological account of HOPE, and the criterion of justified hope). In this chapter, we shall argue—even if we concede, for the sake of argument, that belief that God exists or that there is a life after death would not be epistemically justified —that one could be justified in hoping for these things. We shall argue that the commitments of those who hope that God exists or hope for life after death need not be irrational or unjustified. We shall also defend the (stronger) claim that the morally reasonable person would be entitled to hope for them.

This chapter, then, deals with the epistemological issues. Subsequent chapters consider the *religious adequacy* of a theology resulting from a cognitive   't from belief to hope. There, we shall argue that, although the resultant view may not agree with the prevalent view of ordinary believers, it does offer a robust, even a superior, interpretation of the basic tenets of the Christian religion.

We shall survey the claims of a number of philosophers, not, however, for the sake of textual explication or commentary. We shall evaluate some of their claims and arguments. But however interesting these may be, they are intended primarily to catalyze our own findings.

Kant's Moral Argument

In the *Critique of Pure Reason*, Kant maintains that the problem of God's existence correctly falls under the question, "What may I hope?"[1] Whether or not God exists, he explains, is not decidable by speculative or theoretical reason.[2] It is therefore not appropriately an answer to the question, "What can I know?" Nor is the issue of God's existence simply a practical matter. It is not an answer to the question, "What ought I to do?"

> The . . . question—If I do what I ought to do, what may I then hope?—is at once practical and theoretical, in such fashion that the practical serves only as a clue that leads us to the answer to the theoretical question, and when this is followed out, to the speculative question.[3]

Kant's strategy is to begin with the question of what we may, and morally ought to, hope for. The answer is to provide the basis for the theoretical and speculative questions of God's existence and the immortality of the soul. Kant's conclusion is that we are justified in *postulating* God's existence and the immortality of the soul—postulates required for the vindication of man's moral hope for the "highest good." Clearly, one could not hope—though he could wish idly—for the highest good if he did not at least think its attainment to be logically and/or causally possible. According to Kant, the attainment of the highest good actually requires the existence of God and the immortality of the soul. That is, only on those conditions could the highest good—the situation in which happiness is commensurate with virtue—actually obtain. Hence, if one hopes for the attainment of the highest good—and one is morally obligated to do so—he must, *rationally*, also at least hope, if not believe, that God exists and that men's souls are immortal. Kant maintains, therefore, that belief-in God and the belief-that men's souls are immortal are justified on the basis of our duty to hope for the highest good.

In this section, we shall attempt a reconstruction of part of Kant's argument to the effect that one ought to believe that God exists and that men's souls are immortal. A detailed treatment of Kant's argument would go far beyond the scope of this essay. Hence, only those steps directly related to our central issue will be examined.

From his practical philosophy, Kant concludes that men have a moral obligation to pursue the highest good—that state of affairs in which happiness is commensurate with virtue. If one were to *pursue* that goal (in fact, any goal), he would have at least to believe it not impossible to attain. (That is, when a person, P, rationally pursues a goal, g, P's behavior presupposes that P believes that attainment of g is not impossible.) Conversely, if it is denied by P that g is possible to attain, then P is not in a rational position to pursue g.

For the highest good to obtain, it is necessary (on Kant's view) that God exists and that men's souls are immortal. Suppose, then, that P denies the possibility of the existence of God, or of a future life, or of both. In that case P cannot conceive of the highest good as possible of attainment. But then, given the principle of the relation between belief and action stated earlier, P cannot, as a rational agent pursue the highest good. Of course, if P does not pursue the highest good, then, according to Kant, he is reneging on his *obliga-*

tion to do just that. Hence, by denying that God exists, or that there is a future life, or both, *P* has placed himself in a position in which he cannot rationally pursue the highest good. Since, however, it is his moral obligation to do so, *P* cannot meet his obligation. Hence, *P* is rationally committed to *not denying* that God exists and to *not denying* that there is a future life for man. That is, he is morally obliged to construe them as possibly obtaining.

Of course, the conclusion of this partial reconstruction of Kant's argument is not Kant's conclusion. Kant argues affirmatively that one ought to believe that God exists and that men's souls are immortal. Kant's stronger claim does not follow from our reconstruction. For, not denying God's existence and not denying immortality are compatible with suspending judgment, half-believing, as well as believing, these doctrines to be true.

Our question concerns how Kant could get from the weak conclusion of our reconstruction to his stronger claim. Before turning to this, however, a few points need to be made about the argument leading to the weaker conclusion.

Kant's argument in no way attempts to prove that one must be a moral person. It assumes that one is a moral person, who will, therefore hope for and pursue the highest good. That this is indeed the form of Kant's argument can be seen in the following passage:

> Since, therefore, the moral precept is at the same time my maxim (reason prescribing that it should be so), I inevitably believe in the existence of God and in a future life, and I am certain that nothing can shake this belief, since my moral principles would thereby be themselves overthrown, and I cannot disclaim them without becoming abhorrent in my own eyes.[4]

Clearly Kant maintains that either a person hopes for and pursues the highest good—thereby being committed to "believing in the existence of God and in a future life"— or else he must become "abhorrent in his own eyes." Either one is moral or a scoundrel. The argument is addressed to moral persons. But *if* one is moral, he is rationally committed to a conclusion about God's existence and man's future life. From our reconstruction, however, Kant's argument does *not* commit one to believe positively that God exists or that men are immortal. One is simply committed to not denying these claims.

Kant is fully aware that his argument has force "only for moral beings," that is, only for people who hope for and pursue the highest good. So he says, in the *Critique of Judgment*:

> This moral argument does not supply any *objectively valid* proof of the Being of God; it does not prove to the sceptic that there is a God, but proves that if he wishes to think in a way consonant with morality, he must admit the *assumption* of this proposition under the maxims of his practical reason. We should therefore not say, it is necessary for *morals* [Sittlichkeit] to assume the happiness of all rational beings of the world in proportion to their morality [Moralität] , but rather, this is necessitated *by* morality. Accordingly, this is a *subjective* argument sufficient for moral beings.[5]

The argument is persuasive only "from the inside," that is, only for those who want and pursue the highest good.[6]

Kant, then, considers his moral argument to be "a subjective argument sufficient for moral beings." It is not "objectively sufficient." Propositions derived *via* objectively sufficient arguments are propositions which we *know*. Propositions derived from subjectively sufficient, but objectively insufficient, arguments are propositions we merely *believe* (hold on faith).[7]

> If our holding of the judgment be only subjectively sufficient, and is at the same time taken as being objectively insufficient, we have what is termed *believing* . . . When the holding of a thing to be true is sufficient both subjectively and objectively, it is *knowledge*.[8]

If the proposition "God exists" is known, then one can give an argument for the proposition, based on objective evidence, that the entity in question exists. One has theoretical grounds for holding the proposition. On the other hand, if a proposition is a matter of belief or faith (Glaube), then no theoretical demonstration or evidence for it can be presented. Allen W. Wood offers the following account of faith (Glaube) in Kant:

> Faith, in Kant's view, is essentially different from knowledge, and no theoretical demonstration or even any evidences (Zeugnisse) can be presented in support of judgments which are held in this way. ("What Does it Mean to Orient Oneself in Thought," p. 141) Faith, instead, presupposes that the believer be *conscious* of the "objective insufficiency" of the judgment he holds. (*Ibid.*) Kant anticipates at this point the famous remark of Kierkegaard in the *Concluding Unscientific Postscript*: "If I am capable of grasping God objectively, I do not believe, but precisely because I cannot do this I must believe. If I wish to preserve myself in faith I must constantly be intent upon holding fast to the objective uncertainty, so as to remain out upon the deep, over seventy thousand fathoms of water, still preserving my faith." (p. 182)[9]

The awareness of the "objective insufficiency" of the ground for the propositions in question suggests that faith (as understood here)—just as hope—includes a sense of *uncertainty*, which is not present in the attitude of belief (as "belief" was understood in the chapter on belief and hope).

For Kant, not all "objectively insufficient" beliefs are proper candidates for "subjective" justification. A "subjective" justification is appropriate only in cases in which theoretical cognition is unattainable.[10] If the proposition can be determined by theoretical demonstration to be either true or false, it is not one that can correctly be supported by a subjectively valid argument—for example, the moral argument for God's existence. If the principle of subjective justification is applied to cases that are validly subject to theoretical determination—for example, historical matters—the result is not faith but *credulity*.[11] Kant does not wish to justify credulity.

In "The Ideal of Pure Reason,"[12] Kant maintains that the question of the *possibility* or *impossibility* of God's existence (to be contrasted with the question of God's existence) is a question determinable by pure reason. If the concept of God is either not internally consistent or not consistent with the facts about the world (e.g., the existence of suffering), it is not possible that God exists. However, if the concept of God is both internally consistent and consistent with the facts about the world, it is possible that God exists. In fact, then, it appears to be quite reasonable to maintain that God's existence is possible. We can make a presumption in favor of possibility.

If this alternative is taken, then Kant's "subjective" justification is not correctly applicable to the issue of the possibility or impossibility of God's existence. Nor, of course, is it needed. But Kant wishes to argue for a stronger conclusion than the mere possibility of God's existence. And it may well be that the stronger conclusion, namely, that we ought to believe that God actually exists, is a proposition which is not decidable by pure reason.

Before we deal with the justification of the stronger conclusion, let us see whether the weaker one is adequate for Kant's purposes. Does Kant actually need the stronger conclusion in order that one may rationally hope for, and pursue, the highest good?

In several places, Kant indicates that the weaker conclusion, namely, that God's existence and the future life of man are both *possible*, is sufficient for rationally hoping for and pursuing the highest good. Kant says: "Nothing more is required for this than that he at least cannot pretend that there is any *certainty* that there is *no* such being and *no* such life."[13] The person who hopes for and pursues the highest good will put this minimum condition in a positive rather than a negative way.

A dogmatic *unbelief* cannot subsist together with a moral maxim dominant in the mental attitude (for reason cannot command one to follow a purpose which is cognized as nothing more than a chimera), but a *doubtful faith* can. To this the absence of conviction by grounds of speculative reason is only a hindrance, and for this critical insight into the limits of this faculty can remove its influence upon conduct, while it substitutes by way of compensation a paramount practical belief.[14]

The notion of "doubtful faith" may appear to be a contradiction in terms, like a round square. If faith includes firm belief that something obtains, then doubt is incompatible with faith. However, on the basis of other conceptions—rationally advocated—faith need not be incompatible with doubt. For example, in *Dynamics of Faith*, Paul Tillich claims that "doubt is a necessary element of faith." Faith he understands to be the state of being ultimately concerned. Tillich says that there is necessarily an element of uncertainty or doubt as well as an element of certainty in the attitude of faith.

> Where there is daring and courage there is the possibility of failure. And in every act of faith this possibility is present. The risk must be taken. . . . Only certain is the ultimacy as ultimacy, the infinite passion as infinite passion. This is a reality given to the self with his own nature. . . . But there is not certainty of this kind about the content of our concern, be it nation, success, a god, or the God of the Bible: Their acceptance as matters of ultimate concern is a risk and therefore an act of courage. . . . The risk to faith in one's ultimate concern is indeed the greatest risk a man can run. For if it proves to be a failure, the meaning of one's life breaks down; one surrenders oneself, including truth and justice, to something which is not worth it. . . . If faith is understood as belief that something is true, doubt is incompatible with the act of faith. If faith is understood as being ultimately concerned, doubt is a necessary element in it. It is a consequence of the risk of faith.[15]

Like Tillich, Kant does not understand faith to be the firm belief that something obtains. Thus construed, faith does not enlarge our theoretical knowledge. As Kant understands the notion, faith is a state of mind in which one is aware of the "objective insufficienty" of the grounds for believing that the object of faith obtains. The "objective insufficiency" can result in one's having doubts about whether the object of faith obtains. Yet the state of mind is one of faith since the person continues to pursue his goal, and *acts as if* he were certain that that toward which he aims (as well as that required for what he aims at) obtains.

The notion of faith here outlined is not the faith of the ordinary, traditional theist. The ordinary theist, for whatever reasons, feels *sure* that God exists and that God can be trusted. The ordinary theist's faith is based on what he takes to be a personal relationship between himself and his Creator and Sustainer. In his *Lectures on Ethics,* Kant offers a definition of faith much closer to the ordinary theist's notion. "Faith . . . denotes trust in God that He will supply our deficiency in things beyond our power, provided we have done all within our power."[16] On this definition, there appears to be no doubt about God's existence. Logically, one cannot trust in someone if he does not take it to be beyond reasonable doubt that that person exists.

When Kant says that he has "found it necessary to deny *knowledge* in order to make room for faith,"[17] no doubt the kind of faith he wished to make room for was that of the ordinary believer—presented in the *Lectures*. But how could Kant epistemically justify the move from *doubtful* faith to *trusting* faith?

Kant does not distinguish clearly either (1) the weaker claim (a) that the moral man cannot consistently deny God's existence and the future life from the stronger claim (b) that the moral man must postulate God's existence and the future life; or (2) the weaker notion (a) of doubtful faith from the stronger notion (b) of trusting faith. Hence, Kant fails to deal specifically with moving from the weaker propositions—the most he can derive from our (supposed) moral duty to hope— to the stronger propositions. However, he did wish to argue for the stronger propositions, and he does suggest a possible line of argument for moving from the weaker to the stronger claims.

In order to hope for p, it is necessary that one take p to be possible of attainment. If q must obtain in order that p be possible, then, rationally one must also take q to be possible.

Hence, the possibility of q is all that is logically necessary in order to hope (rationally) that p. However, the actuality of $q-q$ being a necessary condition for p—is required for the fulfillment of one's hope that p. Kant appears to be concerned with what must obtain for these hopes to be fulfilled as well as with what one is rationally committed to if he hopes for the highest good. So he postulates God's existence. How does he justify doing that?

In the *Critique of Practical Reason*, Kant maintains that, in the present case, it is legitimate to move from the hope or want to the objective reality of that which is required for the hope to be fulfilled. Kant says:

> I *will* that there be a God . . . and . . . that my duration be endless; I firmly abide by this, and will not let this faith be taken from me; for in this instance alone my interest, because I *must* not relax anything of it, inevitably determines my judgment. . . .[18]

What Kant is saying is that my want, hope, or interest, namely, the attainment of the highest good, is a moral one. Because my hope for the highest good is a moral duty, I must "promote it with all my powers." The ultimate moral purpose of my life is to promote and pursue the highest good. In order to see the world as a place in which this can be achieved (where my hope is fulfilled), I must hold that there is a God and that my duration is endless; and in order to pursue the highest good "with all my powers," I must see the world as a place in which this purpose *can* be achieved. Hence, in this special circumstance my moral insight is sufficient ground for the determination of my judgment as to what ultimately obtains. Moral insight concerning what we must hope for provides an adequate basis for our judgment concerning objective reality.

In a footnote, Kant underscores the limited scope of the principle whereby one moves from want to reality. A contemporary of his, a Mr. Wizenmann, raised an objection which anticipates an objection made by Sigmund Freud in *Future of an Illusion*. Kant says that Wizenmann disputes the right to argue from a want to the objective reality of its object. . I quite agree with him in this, in all cases where the want is founded on *inclination*. . . . But in the present case we have a want of reason springing from an objective determining principle of the will, namely, the moral law. . . . It is a duty to realize the *summum bonum* to the utmost of our power, therefore it must be possible, consequently it is unavoidable for every rational being in the world to assume what is necessary for its objective possibility.[19]

In evaluating Kant's move, it is important to keep in mind that he places two restrictions on when one can move legitimately from want to objective reality. (1) The question of the objective reality of the object at issue cannot be decided by theoretical reason and demonstration. (2) The objective reality of the object in question is required in order that one actually have as the moral duty the highest good. In this case, one's hope for the highest good is fulfilled only if God exists and there is a future life for men. One cannot have a duty to pursue the highest good if it is unattainable.

Kant's move might be justified psychologically, that is, on the grounds that, in order to pursue the highest good *to the utmost of our power,* it is not enough to hold that it is merely possible that God exists and that there is a future life for men; one must also postulate or assume that they are actual. On this view, one moves from the want to the postulate of the objective reality of the required objects because, with such an attitude one can pursue his moral duty with vigor. One can face setbacks and suffering without falling into despair.

If Kant does have such a defense in mind, at least two strong objections may be raised against it. It is simply not the case that it is necessary to assume God's existence and the future life of man to pursue vigorously one's moral duties— even if the duty to pursue the highest good is among these. If I merely think that the highest good is attainable, and also want it very strongly, I can just as vigorously pursue it as I can if I believe the conditions necessary for the attainment of the highest good do in fact obtain. Of course, if I were convinced that the conditions necessary for the attainment of the highest good did in fact obtain, I would have more reason to persevere, even in the face of setbacks and suffering. But this leads to the second objection.

The postulating of God's existence and of a future life *in order to* pursue one's moral duty with vigor cannot yield the desired result. In fact, it is self-defeating. It is not the postulation that produces the desired state of affairs. It is the *conviction* that the necessary conditions obtain that promotes pursuing one's moral duty with vigor. Postulating something in order to pursue one's goal with vigor does not produce conviction. Hence it appears that one needs some other grounds for persevering, besides one's desire and determination to pursue a supposed possible goal, in order to hold that God exists and that men's souls are immortal.[20] But that there are other rational grounds for this conviction has been denied.

There is, however, another way in which postulating or presuming that God exists and that there is a future life would assist the pursuit of one's moral duty. By merely *entertaining* these possibilities—without actually believing that God exists or that there is a future life, one can visualize more clearly what the world would be like in which one's supposed duty to pursue the highest good were in fact one's duty. If one realized what sort of a world was required in order to vindicate one's hope for the highest good, the strength of one's moral conviction would dispose him to interpret the actual world conformably. Some other interpretation might indeed be the correct one. But in this life at least (since knowledge of these matters is precluded), one could never know which interpretation was actually correct. So, given the Kantian commitment, the interpretation favoring God's existence and the future life would be the best alternative. It would be the interpretation one could most reasonably adopt as a framework within which to live and act. One would be justified in living *as if* the interpretive framework were known to be correct, even though such knowledge is unattainable. Perhaps the state of mind described is what Kant actually has in mind when he says that "in order to believe in God it is not necessary to know for certain that God exists."[21]

As indicated, it is a premise of Kant's argument that we have a moral duty to pursue the highest good. No doubt, many would reject that premise. Lewis White Beck offers the following argument against it. The duty to seek the highest good he claims, does not exist

> as a separate command, independent of the categorical imperative, which is developed without this concept. For suppose I do all in my power—which is all any moral decree can demand of me—to promote the highest good, what am I to do? Simply act out of respect for the law, which I already knew. I can do absolutely nothing else toward apportioning happiness in accordance with desert—that is the task of a moral governor of the universe, not of a laborer in the vineyard. It is not *my* task: my task is to realize the one condition of the *summum bonum* which is within my power.[22]

It seems to me, frankly, that Beck's argument has a great deal of force. Accordingly, we shall adjust our reconstruction of Kant's argument to meet his objection.

Even if it is not one's moral *duty* to pursue—or to want—the highest good, the highest good is certainly something that every (rational) moral person would want. The moral person would hope for the highest good, if he thought it possible to attain. However, on the argument, the highest good is possible only if God exists and there is a future life.

If, by the highest good, we simply mean the end-state in which happiness is commensurate with virtue, then perhaps the highest good is logically possible, whether or not God exists, provided that there is a future life. For example, one can imagine chance combinations of cosmic forces (however remote the likelihood) that produce such a situation. But if the notion of the highest good entails that that state of affairs is a moral or just state of affairs, then God's existence is necessary for the actualization of the highest good. For states of affairs that are just or unjust, moral or immoral, must be brought about by, or obtain as the result of, the activity of one or more intelligent beings. For example, inequality that is merely the result of mere chance cannot be judged unjust. If I am playing bridge and get poor hands all evening, I may have a right to be frustrated and disappointed but, unless I suppose someone to have cheated, I cannot correctly complain of injustice. My fortune is not unjust, it is just unlucky.

On the stronger notion of the highest good, then, God's existence and the future life are necessary that that good obtain. They are, however, not merely the necessary means to the highest good construed as an end. In the stronger sense, God's existence is essentially involved in the very meaning of the "highest good." That is, the highest good (the Kingdom of God) is that state in which happiness is commensurate with virtue *due to* the action of God as a moral agent.

In summary, then, it is reasonable to hold that the highest good is possible, for that which is necessary that the highest good obtain is possible, namely, God's existence and the future life. If the highest good is desired, morally appropriate to desire (which it surely is), and possible, then, on the basis of our account of justifiable hopes (the moral, pragmatic, possibility, and background beliefs tests already mentioned), the hope that the highest good is attainable and the hope that God exists are both justifiable. It appears, then, that it would be rational for the moral person to hope, that is, to keep the door open to the desired possibility by acting as if that for which he longs will obtain. This option now appears to be not very different from Kant's doubtful faith.

Life After Death: An Idle Wish or a Reasonable Hope?

I would like to move, now, farther from the Kantian text and argument to consider the doctrine of life after death. Although we have considered both that doctrine and the thesis of God's existence, our emphasis in the previous section was placed on the question of the possibility of God's existence. Here, the question to be raised concerns whether the hope for a life after death can be justified even if the corresponding belief is not. Inspired by Kant's insights, I will argue that the hope for life after death is a reasonable and justifiable one, not merely an idle wish.

No doubt, there are many reasons why people have believed in, or continue to believe in, life after death. The following may be included: (i) Often, it is a part of one's early religious training which has never been shaken. (ii) In some cases, it is a doctrine inferred from other religious doctrines or beliefs (e.g., God's goodness and power). (iii) Some have had para-normal experiences which they feel can best be explained by appealing to the doctrine of life after death. For example, a medium is said to recount things that "only the dead can have known." (iv) In the face of the death of a loved one, some are unable or unwilling to face the thought of never seeing the departed loved one again. In Gabriel Marcel's play, *Le Mort de Demain*, for instance, Antoine declares, "To love somebody is to say to him, 'You will not die'." If there were a life after death (in the form of personal survival), the loved one could be seen again. (v) In the face of one's own inevitable death, there may be a reluctance to accept one's total annihilation or permanent destruction. Or, one may have a morbid fear of a permanent loss of consciousness. Belief in life after death might calm such fears. (vi) If all ends in death, life may appear (e.g., to Leo Tolstoy) to have no meaning and to be not worth living. So if life is worth living, it may be claimed, there must be life after death. (vii) Only if there is a life after death (in the form of personal survival), it may be thought, could the world be a moral world—in the sense that it could be a place: (1) in which (as Kant holds) one's happiness can be commensurate with one's virtue; and (2) in which justice, love, and beauty can triumph over injustice, cruelty, and ugliness. So if we perceive the world as a moral world, we are committed to a belief in life after death.

This partial list of considerations includes reasons of three types:

(a)   explanations of the origin of some belief (i).
(b)   grounds for the truth of some claim (iii).
(c)   motivation for believing (iv).

Reasons of type (a) are primarily the concern of the psychologist or sociologist of religion. They have no direct bearing on reasons of types (b) and (c).

For the sake of the argument, I readily concede that the usual reasons of type (b) are inadequate for their purpose. They do not provide adequate ground for the truth of the claim that there is life after death.

I should, however, like to consider some of our specific reasons—particularly, (vi) and (vii)—as reasons of type (c). I want to consider whether they provide good reasons *for desiring* life after death. That is, is life after death—in the sense intended in (vi) and (vii)—something one would rationally want? If it is, we should have partially justified the hope in a life after death.

Turn first to (vi) and the question of the relationship between the finality of death and the meaningfulness of life. We may assume, without argument, that everyone desires a meaningful and worthwhile life. Hence, if it were true that life would have no meaning if death ends all, we should have a very good reason for desiring that there be life after death.

But what does it mean for someone's life to have meaning? Perhaps it means that one has intrinsically worthwhile or valuable experiences, for instance, in performing moral actions, experiencing pleasure, mastering an art. There are people, however, (e.g., Leo Tolstoy, as reported in *A Confession*[23]) who meet these conditions and yet find their lives meaningless. One may argue that such people simply are confused, that they have meaningful lives after all. But the argument would hardly be convincing; for, although it may be reasonable to hold that someone who thinks he has a meaningful life does not, it is very odd to insist that someone who sincerely admits not having a meaningful life, does. The reason is simply that believing one's life to be meaningful (I should have thought) is a necessary (though not sufficient) condition for actually having a meaningful life.

What more is required? Consider an analogy. Suppose a person attends a play. He is perplexed by it. He wants to know its meaning. What is he asking for? Apparently he wants to understand the order or "logic" of the drama. What ties it together? A series of funny lines does not make a meaningful or aesthetically valuable comedy. Similarly, a series of intrinsically valuable experiences does not make a meaningful and worthwhile life—contrary to what Antony Flew, Kurt Baier, and others appear to have claimed in recent articles. [24]

There must be some commitment or purpose which brings unity or focus to one's life. One's life needs some unifying direction. Aristotle saw this as one of the necessary conditions of maturity. Both Søren Kierkegaard and Paul Tillich stress the importance of a centered life, in which one "wills one thing" or in which one has an "ultimate concern." The question then becomes what is worthy of one's ultimate concern. What could be of sufficient value to become the focal point of one's entire activity? It seems that each person must develop a self-concept and commit himself to something that he takes to be worthy of such commitment. Just as alternative themes may serve as the focal point of a good drama—though not every theme—so, too, many different concerns may be of sufficient power to center one's life. Certainly it seems reasonable that different objectives and interests would be appropriate for different people, given their various abilities and dispositions.

Finding one's own concern and pursuing it is what is meant by self-fulfillment. Viewing the pursuit of one's goals as a fulfillment of oneself is required for one's life to be meaningful. Hence, if one's life is to be meaningful, the achievement of the self-fulfillment to which one is committed must be taken to be possible.

It is that requirement that brings the question of the meaning of one's life into confrontation with the fact of death. It seems to me that the "arrest of life," of which Tolstoy speaks, arises when genuine self-fulfillment no longer appears possible. As Teilhard de Chardin says:

> An animal may rush headlong down a blind alley or towards a precipice. Man will never take a step in a direction he knows to be blocked. There lies precisely the ill that causes our disquiet. [25]

The road ahead must be seen to be open. As in Tolstoy's case, if one perceives that death blocks one's road to fulfillment, one cannot go on. Teilhard continues:

> Hence this remarkable situation—that our mind, by the very fact of being able to discern infinite horizons ahead, is only able to move by the hope of achieving, through something of itself, a supreme consummation—without which it would rightly feel itself to be stunted, frustrated and cheated. By the nature of the work, and correlatively by the requirement of the worker, a total death, and unscalable wall, on which consciousness would crash and then forever disappear, are thus "incompossible" with the mechanism of conscious activity (since it would immediately break its mainspring). [26]

Unless one's sense of self and one's potential are very limited or one is uncommonly blessed with favorable conditions and knows it, death blocks one's path to genuine fulfillment. It is a thief coming unexpectedly in the night. At the time of one's death, self-fulfillment normally has not been attained. Much of one's potential remains untapped. If, then death is the final curtain, it destroys the possibility of a truly meaningful life to a great many. For them, it would be reasonable to desire a life after death in the form of personal survival.

Obviously, not just any form of extended life serves the purpose of providing one's life with meaning. The argument presupposes a conception in which the conditions for continued self-development would be optimal. Traditional religions have speculated about what such a life would be like. H. H. Price's "Survival and the Idea of 'Another World'" is also helpful.[27] However, we need not attempt here to work out the details of such an after-life. The argument does not require them.

Let us suppose that life after death of the appropriate sort is desirable for at least certain people. If we *knew* that life after death was not possible, then, although it might be desirable, it could not be an appropriate object of hope. But, as far as I know, there is no convincing demonstration of the impossibility of personal survival. Such a demonstration would consist either of a proof of the logical inconsistency of the notion of personal survival or a proof of the incompatibility of our contemporary scientific understanding of human death and the thesis of personal survival.

As previously mentioned, H. H. Price has speculated about what after-death experiences would be like. There may not be any such experiences, but he presents a possible "other world" which one would be hard pressed to show is logically inconsistent. It is, in fact, a readily imaginable world.

Modern scientific views of the self and of death doubtless weaken the plausibility of certain traditional arguments for the truth of the proposition, "There is a life after death." But can it be demonstrated that the hypothesis is actually *incompatible with* such an understanding? William James' response to this question, in 1893, is still appropriate today. Suppose psychophysiology established that "thought is a function of the brain."[28] If we wondered whether affirming that thesis compelled us to deny the possibility of life after death, we should have to examine the concept of "function" more carefully. If "function" signified (an essential) *productive* function as in "steam is a function of the teakettle," or "light is a function of the electric circuit"—then decay of the brain would entail the end of thought, *a fortiori*, the impossibility of personal survival of bodily death. But if "function" signified a releasing or *transmissive* function (that could be variably manifested), we would not be forced to the same conclusion. The trigger of a crossbow has a releasing function. A colored glass, a prism, a reflecting lens have transmissive functions. If the brain performs a transmissive function, it does not follow from the claim that "thought is a function of the brain" that destruction of the brain results in destruction of the thought.[29] James goes on to argue that it is at least equally plausible to see the brain's function as transmissive as it is to see it as productive.[30]

However, even if one supposed that thought was destroyed by the decay of the brain, it would still not follow that life after death was impossible. Perhaps—as certain Jewish and Christian theologies have maintained—people die but are resurrected later and given new "spiritual bodies." I doubt that the notion of resurrection is inconsistent.[31] It seems to be imaginable. If consistent, it is not a possibility that science can ignore. Science may claim correctly that there is no evidence in its favor. But that is a far weaker charge.

These issues have been widely debated. My own remarks were not intended to add anything new; they were intended rather to fix certain reasons for maintaining that life after death in the form of personal survival is possible.

I want to consider briefly, before applying the test for justified hope to the hope for life after death, one of the reasons listed above—(vii), the desire for a moral world. If it were a matter of choice, a moral person would choose a world in which justice, love and beauty prevailed over injustice, hatred and ugliness. Of course, we are not called upon to make such a choice. Instead, we find ourselves thrown into a world in which the wicked often prosper and enjoy longevity, while the righteous suffer and die early and ignominious deaths. Given this distressing empirical fact, it is clear that if the happiness of individuals is to be commensurate with their virtue—if justice is to win out ultimately—human life cannot end at the grave.

If we accept as axiomatic the Kantian maxim that each human being is to be valued as an end and not as a means only (i.e., as having intrinsic worth and the right to strive for his own fulfillment), then we must desire the possibility of fulfillment for all human beings. Nevertheless, for the vast majority of mankind—including the victims of Auschwitz, the napalmed babies of Vietnam, the starving millions of East Africa—life is plainly brutish, repressive, and short. Only a very few (e.g., some few members of the wealthy leisure class, the specially gifted, the educated elite, the lucky) find it actually possible to control their own lives (and not to be merely means to another's ends). Only if there were personal survival after death, would the *possibility* exist that all persons could have the opportunity to strive for their own genuine fullfillment. One might certainly wish that the world were more amenable to the needs and aspirations of mankind. (One may wish, but not hope, counterfactually.) Still, given the human condition and the limits of our knowledge, one may hope that reality is greater than appearance, that the visible world is actually enveloped in an unseen larger world. For then, it would be possible that (for every individual) justice could conquer injustice; love, hate; the forces of life and fulfillment, those of death and destruction.

I have confined our discussion to one form of life after death and to a few reasons for believing in life after death. But let us, within those constraints, consider whether the hope for life after death meets the requirements for justified hope.

Given the reasons (cited above), certainly the moral test is satified. For example, the desire for a moral world is clearly a proper desire. This is not to say that it would not be possible for someone to desire life after death for morally unworthy reasons—e.g., a desire to see non-believers suffer. But it is to say that one's desire need not be ignoble or even selfish.

The desire for a meaningful life, for the possibility of ultimate self-fulfillment, is clearly compatible with all or most of one's other desires. In fact, it provides the way in which such desires are normally brought together in a unified whole. As has been argued, an appropriate sort of life after death would be a possible means by which such meaning and fulfillment could be actualized. Hence, the hope for life after death meets the pragmatic test.

I have already indicated that there is at least a strong presumption that the hope for life after death would meet the possibility test. If the arguments already collected are correct, then the background beliefs test would also be satisfied. Even so, if there were little at stake, and if the possibility of life after death seemed very remote, the desire for life after death would remain no more than an idle wish. However, if much were at stake—and there is a great deal at stake, as the arguments presented demonstrate—then, despite the fact that it remains no more than a possibility (certainly not a probability), the desire for life after death must be admitted to be a reasonable hope.

Strength of desire coupled with strength of favorable evidence determines the appropriate strength of hope. Hence, even though the favorable evidence is not strong (which we have conceded, regarding life after death), if the strength of the desire were justifiably strong, it would be reasonable for one's hope to be quite strong (i.e., the combined strength of the evidence and the desire).

I have then presented a test for justified hopes, and have offered some reasons for believing that the hope for life after death can meet these tests. Much more could, and perhaps should, be said about this matter. But to my mind, even these initial reflections point to an affirmative answer: the hope for a life after death appears to be justifiable. I conclude that it *is* a reasonable hope, not merely an idle wish. One *is* justified in keeping the door open to the desired possibility, in spite of the lack of any firm evidence in its favor.

Schopenhauer and Freud: The Counsel to Resign

In the next few sections, we shall examine some possible arguments against the defense of the right to hope for God's existence and an afterlife. The most powerful objections may well follow Arthur Schopenhauer's and Sigmund Freud's attack on religion.

Schopenhauer felt that the enlightenment of the Stoic sage represented "the highest point to which man can attain by the mere use of his faculty of reason."[32] According to

Schopenhauer, the Stoic sage realized that

> . . . want and suffering did not result directly and necessarily from not having, but only from desiring to have and yet not having; that this desiring to have is therefore the necessary condition under which alone not having becomes privation and engenders pain. . . . Moreover, it was recognized from experience that it is merely the hope, the claim, which begets and nourishes the wish. . . . Every wish soon dies and so can beget no more pain, if no hope nourishes it. . . . All suffering really results from the want of proportion between what we demand and expect and what comes to us. [33]

Schopenhauer speaks of "the allurement of hope,"[34] claiming that "hope bribes us."[35]

> Most common of occurrence is the falsification of knowledge brought about by desire and hope, since they show us the scarcely possible in dazzling colours as probable and well-nigh certain, and render us almost incapable of comprehending what is opposed to it.[36]

Later, in *The World as Will and Representation,* he explicitly says:

> *Hope* makes us regard what we desire, and *fear* what we are afraid of, as being probable or near, and both magnify their object. . . . Hope's nature lies in the fact that the will, when its servant, the intellect, is unable to produce the thing desired, compels this servant at any rate to picture this thing to it, and generally to undertake the role of comforter, to pacify its lord and master, as a nurse does a child, with fairy-tales, and to deck these out so that they obtain an appearance of verissimilitude. Here the intellect is bound to do violence to its own nature, which is aimed at truth, since it is compelled, contrary to its own laws, to regard as true things that are neither true nor probable, and often scarcely possible, merely in order to pacify, soothe, and send to sleep for a while the restless and unmanageable will.[37]

In these passages, Schopenhauer practically maintains that hope is the root of mankind's basic problem, namely, interference with one's attaining the goal of deep tranquility—freedom from pain, suffering, anxiety. Hope is the double evil: (i) it beguiles the mind, and clouds one's vision of reality; (ii) it insidiously gives one false expectations, and prepares one for the inevitable and profound disappointment that follows one's realization that the gap between desire and what the world can offer cannot be bridged. What Schopenhauer recommends, therefore, is to resist the temptation to hope and to develop in its place the Stoic attitude of resignation.

Consider Schopenhauer's case. Against his first criticism (that hope clouds one's vision of reality) we have in effect established that it is neither a logical nor a psychological *necessity* that hope negatively affect one's perception of reality. Thus, one may hope that p and be as clear as the next, of the odds against p.

It is true that, since, in hoping for p one desires that p and is disposed to act as if p, there is a danger (in hoping) that one may allow his judgment to be affected. Plato rightly warns us, in *Timaeus*, that hope leads one astray easily (69d). However, it does not follow that if a particular path has its dangers it ought not to be used. Obviously, the automobile, nuclear energy, space travel, psychological and genetic research all have their dangers and may even be turned to evil uses. Yet these are hardly regarded as sufficient reasons to discontinue their use and development. Only if such dangers could not be counterbalanced by suitable positive contributions would their suppression be thought reasonable. Schopenhauer apparently felt that a case for hope's positive contribution could not be made out. I, of course, have opposed that thesis.

Admittedly, hope entails risk. In acting hopingly one cannot wait for the conclusive evidence. One must take chances in favor of the alternative preferred. But one does so, rationally *fully cognizant* of that risk. Doubtless, many would be unable to live with such uncertainty. The tension would be too much. They might even claim that it was preferable to give up one's hope for the seemingly unattainable goal of self-fulfillment and the highest good. They might be willing to resign themselves to a lesser objective—securing a measure of certainty and a resolution of the tension of constant striving. I shall, however (discussing William James, below), argue that such a trade off is not a rational alternative.

Sigmund Freud, whose critique of religion was directly influenced by Schopenhauer,[38] mounts a somewhat similar argument. In *The Future of an Illusion* his attack on religion is specifically directed against belief rather than hope; but the sense of his argument is clear enough—religious hopes are to be condemned. Freud follows Schopenhauer in counselling *resignation* rather than the "illusion" of hope. Resignation to reality, he says—submitting every desire to the hard test of reality—is the only rational and mature course to adopt. We must abandon our desire for objects not favored by our perception of the apparent world.

> Men cannot remain children forever, they must in the end go out into "hostile life." We may call this *"education to reality."* Need I confess to you that the sole purpose of my book is to point out the necessity for this forward step?[39]

The principal difficulty with Freud's counsel of resignation is just that it rests on an unwarranted assumption about the nature of reality. It assumes that we know what lies behind appearances, what reality actually is—or at best that we need pursue the matter no further. But it is presumptuous to maintain, without proof, that one knows either that God exists or does not or that there is or is no life after death. The difficulty, precisely, is that we cannot know. Certainly, such knowledge cannot be had by applying the methods of science. Freud merely refuses to countenance any other cognitive source. Hence, it is not fully consistent with his scepticism to maintain that he can penetrate behind appearances to assure us that there is no God and no afterlife.

If we could be absolutely certain that Freud's nontheistic, this-worldly perspective captured the whole of reality, his claim that religious hopes were based on infantile desires, that they represented a deep inability to confront reality as it actually is, would be entirely persuasive. For then, our hopes would run counter to reality, would constitute a way of hiding from reality. In that case, they ought to be condemned as immature. The mature thing, then would be to "resign" oneself to reality, in spite of the sad fact that reality fails to conform to our wishes and our aspirations.

Those who counsel hope depend on the fact that we cannot know whether reality vindicates our hopes: in that situation, proponents maintain that it is best to keep the door open to the favorable option. They see no need to make things out to be worse than they possibly are. And they are willing to live with the risk and uncertainty entailed. What concerns Freud, rather, is the deception, the intellectual dishonesty, he imagines he finds in one's subscribing to religious beliefs. Certainly, the charge applies in many cases. Unfounded religious dogmatism is frequent enough.

> Ignorance is ignorance; no right to believe anything can be derived from it. In other matters no sensible person will behave so irresponsibly or rest content with such feeble grounds for his opinions and for the line he takes. . . . Where questions of religion are concerned, people are guilty of every possible sort of dishonesty and intellectual misdemeanour.[40]

As an empirical observation, Freud's remark is unobjectionable. But it hardly follows that the only basis for harboring religious hopes must be irresponsible and immature. In earlier sections, we have already shown how to construct a basis for such hopes that is neither epistemically, morally, nor pragmatically dubious. We simply need not believe irresponsibly or immaturely.

The source of these alternative attitudes toward religious hope lies in a different conception of desires. Freud is suspicious of wishes and desires. He counsels "renunciation of instincts."[41] We must, he insists, hold suspect—if we need not actually deny—any thought in which a wish-fulfillment is a prominent factor. Desires are wishes which arise from the blind irrationality of the instinctual life of the human organism. The proponent of hope does not subscribe to such a negative attitude. He entertains, instead, the possibility that our desires provide us with a clue about the nature of reality itself.

Of course, in religion, wants and desires cannot but play an extremely important role. The origin of religious beliefs, Freud says, are the "strongest and most urgent wishes of mankind."[42]

> It would be very nice if there were a God who created the world and was a benevolent Providence, and if there were a moral order in the universe and an after-life; but it is a very striking fact that all this is exactly as we are bound to wish it to be.[43]

But he goes on to claim, unjustifiably, that they must be discounted as *illusions*.

Here, Freud offers a position that we have a strong initial inclination to accept. The proponent of hope, however, finds no valid grounds for adopting it exclusively. It is, he supposes an over-reaction to the fear of disappointment. We often say of something that it is too good to be true. One naturally discounts or denies possibilities one has hardly dared to dream might come true. Kierkegaard illustrates this tendency in his parable about the day-laborer and the mightiest Emperor that ever lived. He asks us to imagine an Emperor sending for a poor man who would think that he didn't even know of his existence, who would suppose himself fortunate "if merely he was permitted once to see the Emperor [so that he] would [be able to] recount it to his children and children's children as the most important event of his life." The Emperor informs the laborer that he wishes to have him for his son-in-law.

> The laborer, humanly, would become somewhat or very much puzzled, shame-faced, and embarrassed, and it would seem to him, quite humanly (and this is the human element in it), something exceedingly strange, something quite mad, the last thing in the world about which he would say a word to anybody else, since he himself in his own mind was not far from explaining it by supposing (as

his neighbors would be busy doing as soon as possible) that the Emperor wanted to make a fool of him, so that the poor man would be the laughing-stock of the whole town, his picture in the papers, the story of his espousal to the Emperor's daughter the theme of ballad-mongers. This thing, however, of becoming the Emperor's son-in-law might readily be subjected to the tests of reality. . . . And suppose now that this was not an external reality but an inward thing, so that factual proofs could not help the laborer to certitude . . . how many laboring men were there likely to be who possessed this courage? But he who had not this courage would be offended; the extraordinary would seem to him almost like mockery of him. He would then perhaps honestly and plainly admit, "Such a thing is too high for me, I cannot get it into my head; it seems to me, if I may blurt it straight out, foolishness.[44]

Freud says that a belief is an illusion "when a wish-fulfillment is a prominent factor in its motivation."[45] As one expects, according to Freud, illusions must be rejected, in spite of the fact that Freud himself concedes that, on this definition, illusions "need not necessarily be false."[46] Contrary to ordinary usage,[47] in Freud's sense, that a proposition is an illusion does not justify denying its truth. Hence, we must ask William James' question: if the proposition, "There is an afterlife" may actually be true, and if it would, if true, enrich, or give meaning to, one's life, why should one be denied the right to hope for, or to pursue, or to keep the door open to, that desired possibility? Freud's policy seems unwise even in the context of the sciences.

Doubtless, one's own desires ought to play a minimum role within the practices of an ideal science. A laboratory technician must learn to suppress his own biases, must allow his experiments to run their course unimpeded. His procedures will be undermined if he fails to obey the ground rule about keeping one's hope for favorable results from affecting one's work. But the rule applies to the *testing* of hypotheses and theories; it hardly applies to the work of *discovery*. The processes of discovery are not techniques that can be neatly delineated by procedural discipline. Discovery often requires breaking out of established disciplines, usual procedures, accepted theories, received views of what is real and what is possible, daring to leave the security of what is known and verified in order to pursue a hunch or a dream or a hope down unknown paths. James Watson's account of the discovery of the structure of DNA—one of the signal accomplishments of our century[48] —confirms the point in the most vivid way.

Also, recent work in the philosophy of science demonstrates the inadequacy of conceiving of science primarily in terms of the mere testing of hypotheses and theories. Michael Polanyi flatly asserts that ". . . complete objectivity as usually attributed to the exact sciences is a delusion and is in fact a false ideal."[49]

> The prevailing conception of science . . . seeks—and must seek at all costs—to eliminate from science such passionate, personal, human appraisals of theories, or at least to minimize their function to that of a negligible by-play. For modern man has set up as the ideal of knowledge the conception of natural science as a set of statements which is "objective" in the sense that its substance is entirely determined by observation, even while its presentation may be shaped by convention.[50]

A clearer picture of scientific activity confirms the sense in which a person's wishes form an essential component of the processes of discovery.

> The application of existing rules can produce valuable surveys, but does not advance the principles of science. We have to cross the logical gap between a problem and its solution by relying on the unspecifiable impulse of our heuristic passion, and must undergo as we do so a change of our intellectual personality. Like all ventures in which we comprehensively dispose of ourselves, such an intentional change of our personality requires a passionate motive to accomplish it. Originality must be passionate.[51]

Contrary, then, to Freud's implied view, wish-fulfillment and risk-taking are essential aspects of scientific advancement. We cannot, in this respect, oppose the scientific and religious perspectives. As Polanyi says, science as well as religion requires an act of hope.

> Intellectual commitment is a responsible decision, in submission to the compelling claims of what in good conscience I conceive to be true. It is an act of hope, striving to fulfill an obligation within a personal situation for which I am not responsible and which therefore determines my calling. This hope and this obligation are expressed in the universal intent of personal knowledge.[52]

So the history of science bears us out that wishes and desires play an ineliminable role in the processes of discovery. Even the alchemists' wish to turn base metals into gold opened the way to discoveries that would otherwise have been postponed or lost. Hence, we should emphasize the importance of "wish-fulfillment" for science, rather than repudiate it, with Freud.

This William James has done. In his "Is Life Worth Living?", James strongly supports the heuristic role of wishes and intellectual passions.

> Is it not sheer dogmatic folly to say that our inner interests can have no real connection with the forces that the hidden world may contain? . . . Without an imperious inner demand on our part for ideal logical and mathematical harmonies, we should never have attained to proving that such harmonies lie hidden between all the chinks and interstices of the crude natural world.
>
> Hardly a law has been established in science, hardly a fact ascertained, which was not first sought after, often with sweat and blood, to gratify an inner need. . . . If needs of ours outrun the visible universe, why *may* not that be a sign that an invisible universe is there? [53]

If we take James's cue, it is the discovery rather than the testing stage of science that most resembles the projection of religious hopes. Of course religious propositions are not testable. The wishes for a technician intruding on his tests *invalidates* his work. But desires that inform one's search for a new theory or a new interpretation of one's data in no way counts against its *possible truth*.

It is ironic that Freud, whose work was so clearly guided by the hope and belief that psychoanalysis could assist mankind to a happier and more mature life, opposed the legitimacy of religious hopes intended in a cognate purpose. In neither case is there conclusive (possibly not even strong) evidence in favor of the hopes or beliefs posited. What evidence could there have been in Freud's time that mankind would become truly rational, or that all social problems would be solved by the skills of scientific engineering? If anything, the evidence pointed in the opposite direction. Only a small band of the enlightened, atheistic elite could be counted on to redeem the masses suffering from ignorance, neuroses, and the greatest disorder of all—religious faith.

Where is the progress of the last hundred years due to the science of psychoanalytic counselling? How far from the mark that hope now appears.

Still, whatever progress has been made entailed the bold hopes of Freud and likeminded scientists against the odds of easy confirmation. These, of course, are just the cases in which "wish-fulfillment" plays a decisive role. Nor should we deny science the right to such hopes. They meet, in fact, our criteria for justified *hopes*. But since religious hopes do so as well, it cannot but be prejudicial to treat them as unjustified simply because they are concerned with religious matters rather than scientific.

Freud opposes religion and the scientific ethic of "resignation." But this presents us with a false option. The activity of science itself is inseparable from hopes of the sort Freud harbored. At best, "resignation" is applicable to the testing stage of science. It can only stifle the stage of discovery. If religious hopes need not be signs of arrested development, or premised on false beliefs, or directed toward objects known to be non-existent, then Freud's objections simply collapse.

Camus' Rebellion

Jean-Paul Sartre said, ". . . there is no God and no prevenient design which can adapt the world and all its possibilities to my will." Hence, "we should act without hope."[54] Reacting to Sartre's position, Albert Camus maintained that such ontological despair, or nausea, was a position which could not be consistently held by anyone who did not end his life by suicide. To survive, one needs to go beyond ontological despair to ontological or metaphysical rebellion. Camus says that "the metaphysical rebel declares that he is frustrated by the universe."[55] But the metaphysical rebel, protesting against "the incompleteness of human life, expressed by death, and its dispersion, expressed by evil,"[56] realizes that one must create values and order oneself,[57] without reference to any supposed cosmic values or cosmic order. Hope for ultimate justice, ultimate order and unity, will inevitably be frustrated. But, in protest, some hope at least of the fulfillment of one's created values is possible.

In *The Myth of Sisyphus*, Camus says that we must not take the leap toward the transcendent. We must cease to hope. Hope is "the typical act of eluding,"[58] our way of fending off reality. Like Freud, Camus is determined to face reality, no matter how brutal, ugly, disagreeable, chaotic, or absurd.

> My reasoning wants to be faithful to the evidence that aroused it. That evidence is the absurd. It is that divorce between the mind that desires and the world that disappoints, my nostalgia for unity, this fragmented universe and the contradiction that binds them together.[59]

Camus calls himself and those who remain faithful to the evidence, absurd men. What the absurd man "demands of himself is to live *solely* with what he knows, to accomodate himself to what is, and to bring in nothing that is not certain . . . he wants to find out if it is possible to live without appeal."[60] Only a few certainties remain.

> And these two certainties—my appetite for the absolute and for unity and the impossibility of reducing this world to a rational and reasonable principle—I also know that I cannot reconcile them. What

other truth can I admit without lying, without bringing in a hope I lack and which means nothing within the limits of my condition?[61]

For both Camus and Freud, hopes are illusions. For Freud, the trouble is that we harbor hopes and beliefs for which we have no right. Hence, they must be expelled. Sometimes, Camus appears to say the same thing. But at other times, his position is quite different. Being honest with himself, he finds that he has no transcendent hopes, no hopes that the world will satisfy our needs. Camus has *given up* hopes of that sort. He believes he is not alone in this: the loss of hope is a phenomenon of our time. "[I]n a universe suddenly divested of illusions and lights, man feels an alien, a stranger. His exile is without remedy since he is deprived of the memory of a lost home or the hope of a promised land."[62] We simply delude ourselves if we act as if we had such a hope.

The only honest, potentially noble thing to do is to rebel— to stand up to the world's indifference and failure to meet our needs—to make the best of a hopeless situtation. Suicide, which some might consider a better alternative, is an unacceptable alternative because it is unmanly.

It is essential to die unreconciled and not of one's own free will. Suicide is a repudiation. The absurd man can only drain everything to the bitter end, and deplete himself. The absurd is his extreme tension, which he maintains constantly by solitary effort, for he knows that in that consciousness and in that day-to-day revolt he gives proof of his only truth, which is defiance.[63]

Honesty and pride require that we remain unreconciled, that we do not acquiesce.

In contrast to Nietzsche, Camus feels that it would be a good thing if God did exist.

The certainty of a God giving a meaning to life far surpasses in attractiveness the ability to behave badly with impunity. The choice would not be hard to make. But there is no choice, and that is where the bitterness comes in. [64]

God's existence is desirable. The trouble is that He doesn't exist. In a godless world, there can be no reconciliation. What would be required, Camus says, is a world responsive to our needs. "If man realized that the universe like him can love and suffer, he would be reconciled."[65] It is not sufficient that things may work out for the best one way or another. The process must be of a special sort; the cosmic forces must be in communion with us. But they are not, and the search for such responsiveness would only be disappointed. Knowing that, to search on would be a sham. We must stand up and refuse to take part any longer. We must rebel.

Camus makes a very moving appeal. All of us, at times, have been disappointed by failure of the world to meet our needs and desires. For some, this may have been a bitter disappointment. But it is then that we feel the need to rebel. Had we thought of God as working, within nature, to meet our individual needs, we should have rebelled. For such a God would have failed us. Hence, there is no God.

Coolly considered, however, the same criticisms leveled against Freud quite clearly apply against Camus. For example, how does Camus know that the appearance of indifference reveals the truth? How does he know that what he sees and experiences is all there is, that there is nothing beyond these appearances? He offers no compelling argument. (Doubtless, he never intended to.)

One must admire Camus' sense of honesty. Whatever the reasons, Camus believes the world can sustain hope no longer: the highest good, even order and rationality, are out of reach. God's existence would of course support a far more attractive commitment. But that hope is doomed. So, rather than be unfaithful to his own perception and instinct, he takes his stand in this godless, absurd world.

James, whose analysis of our situation is rather similar to Camus', offers a very different solution. Paralleling the account of the absurd, James holds that the source of our uneasiness is "the contradiction between the phenomena of nature and the craving of the heart."[66] We crave "communion with the total soul of things." But the world disappoints us in this. Inner discord and contradiction result. He recognizes two ways to relieve our tension: "The longing to read the facts religiously may cease, and leave the bare facts by themselves; or, supplementary facts may be discovered or believed-in, which permit the religious reading to go on."[67] Camus favors the first alternative; James adopts the second.

But James seems to feel that the first alternative (in effect, Camus') is preparatory—possibly even a necessary first step—for the second. He says that "the initial step towards getting into healthy ultimate relations with the universe is the act of rebellion against the idea that . . . God (conceived of as the God of nature) exists."[68] The God who is the proper object of hope must be a God above such a God.

Before examining James' alternative, however, we must consider two issues that have been touched on. (i) Camus maintains (as do Schopenhauer and Freud) that the existence of the Judeo-Christian God would be desirable. The trouble is that the evidence is against it—or at least unfavorable. His contention, therefore, conforms with the view of the theologian of hope—which Nietzsche, in effect, finds quite undesirable. We shall have to consider Nietzsche's dissenting opinion. (ii) Camus suggests that the loss of hope is a phenomenon of our time. But if we have lost the capacity to hope for "the promised land," or an afterlife, the alternative pressed in this essay will have little application. It will be helpful, therefore, in thinking about the matter, to consult Ernst Bloch's magnum opus, *Das Prinzip Hoffnung*.

Nietzsche's Dissent

Friedrich Nietzsche clearly claims to have found the existence of God undesirable; conversely, the "death of God," or the decline of the belief-in God desirable.

> The greatest recent event—that "God is dead," that the belief in the Christian God has ceased to be believable—is even now beginning to cast its first shadows over Europe. . . . We philosophers and "free spirits" feel as if a new dawn were shining on us when we receive the

tidings that "the old god is dead"; our heart overflows with grati-
tude, amazement, anticipation, expectation. At last the horizon
appears free again to us, even granted that it is not bright; at last our
ships may venture out again, venture out to face any danger; all the
daring of the lover of knowledge is permitted again; the sea, *our* sea,
lies open again; perhaps there never yet has been such an "open
sea." [69]

Nietzsche speaks about how the belief in God has, or at
least should have been overcome. Truth-seekers are to concern themselves only with "what is thinkable for man, visible
for man, feelable by man." He continues:

And how would you bear life without this hope, you lovers of
knowledge? You could not have been born either into the incomprehensible or into the irrational.
But let me reveal my heart to you entirely, my friends: *if* there
were gods, how could I endure not to be a god! *Hence* there are no
gods. Though I drew this conclusion, now it draws me. [70]

According to Nietzsche, the decay of the belief-in God
opens the way for the full development of man's creative
energy. ". . . a 'God' and total sensorium would altogether be
something on account of which life would have to be condemned—Precisely that we have eliminated the total consciousness that posited ends and means, is our great relief—
with that we are no longer *compelled* to be pessimists—Our
greatest *reproach* against existence was the *existence of
God.*" [71]

What alone can be our doctrine? That no one *gives* man his qualities
—neither God, nor society, nor his parents and ancestors, nor he
himself. . . . That nobody is held responsible any longer, that the
mode of being may not be traced back to a *causa prima*, that the
world does not form a unity either as a sensorium or a "spirit"—that
alone is the great liberation; with this alone is the innocence of becoming restored. The concept of "God" was until now the greatest
objection to existence. We deny God, we deny the responsibility in
God: only thereby do we redeem the world. [72]

The god of commands and prohibitions—the god *hostile* to life—no longer blocks the way.

> The Christian conception of God—God as god of the sick, God as a spider, God as spirit—is one of the most corrupt conceptions of the divine ever attained on earth. . . . God degenerated into the *contradiction* of life, instead of being its transfiguration and eternal Yes![73]

With this god's demise, the door to the future lies open. The new atheism makes room for a life of strength, intelligence, creativity, concern for the future of man. We are free, for now the world is ours—to make rather than to discover. We are the center and the lawgivers. Now, we can live in tune with what really matters.

> These small things—nutrition, place, climate, recreation, the whole casuistry of selfishness—are inconceivably more important than everything one has taken to be important so far. Precisely here one must begin to *relearn*. What mankind has so far considered seriously have not even been realities but mere imaginings—more strictly speaking, *lies* prompted by the bad instincts of sick natures that were harmful in the most profound sense—all these concepts, "god," "soul," "virtue," "sin," "beyond," "truth," "eternal life."[74]

Nietzsche's greatness lies in his ability to see issues from an entirely new vantage. He not only announces the death of God. He affirms it to be a good. For, now (i) life can be a venture; (ii) the way is cleared for the uninhibited expression of our creative power; and (iii) "life" itself can be celebrated.

(i) In *The Gay Science,* Nietzsche says, "The secret of the greatest fruitfulness and the greatest enjoyment of existence is: to live dangerously.[75] If God is "dead," the future is open. The restrictions, the prohibitions, the guilt, the fear of transgressing—inhibitors against setting out on a venture of one's own making—can be swept away.

Reading Nietzsche, one responds to his compelling style, shares with him the elation, the relief, the full realization that one need struggle no longer under the yoke of a jealous, vindictive, and punitive taskmaster. If *such a God* is dead—no longer the concern of modern man—if the future is really open, then Nietzsche is right to celebrate. The theologian of hope will celebrate as well, for he also believes that the "death" of that God is cause of joy, and that an open future and a life of venture are to be welcomed. They part, however, about the requirments of such a life.

(ii) In contrast to Nietzsche, the theologian of hope maintains that God's existence—correctly understood and freed of the offensive and extraneous attributes so often ascribed to God (and so tellingly observed by Nietzsche)—would actually guarantee the open future desired. This has, of course, been the essential point of an earlier argument favoring the right to hope that God exists and the possibility of an afterlife.

(iii) Whereas the theologian of hope wishes an open future for the sake of actualizing the traditional individual and collective values of Western culture, Nietzsche defends a much more radical position. He means to undermine essential Judeo-Christian values, for, on his view, they glorify weakness of body and spirit and mind rather than strength and creativity. He does not hope (as we have hoped) that justice, for example—a virtue of the weak—will triumph. Nietzsche pursues a new "morality," a conviction to take us beyond good and evil and back to the life of the senses (as advertised in the passage cited from *Ecce Homo*). It would take us too far afield to determine whether it ought actually to be favored. Clearly, in accord with our Kantian argument, anyone who repudiates morality or chooses a life "beyond" morality, has found a way around this essay's argument. It seems very unlikely, however, that many would find Nietzsche's new "morality" compelling. I am content, therefore, to rest the case here as before—on the thesis that the arguments advanced can persuade only those who desire to be moral. For such, God's existence and an afterlife are objects of hope and desire.

Bloch's Principle of Hope

Ernst Bloch, a contemporary German Marxist, has, through his phenomenological studies, found within man a deep and irrepressible propensity to hope. He claims, in fact, that *the key* to understanding human existence may be found in the very hopes man holds for the future state of humanity and the world. Man realizes himself in projects: he *is* the creature that hopes. To be human *is* to dream about the future, to act in the present in order to bring about that which is "not yet" ("noch nicht"). Rather than "thinker," or "tool maker," or "symbol maker," man, for Bloch, is the creature that hopes. He lives and acts with an abiding sense of *possibilities* that may be, and are not yet, realized.

Bloch demonstrates that, today, as in the past, men have always harbored transcendent hopes. In *Das Prinzip Hoffnung*, his massive work on hope, Bloch painstakingly identifies and documents such objects of hope as the full life,[76] the perfect life,[77] the world without disappointment,[78] peace, freedom, bread,[79] and above all, the highest good.[80]

If, as Camus maintains, it appears that man today lacks any hopes of the sort that Bloch lists, we may suspect that it may be due to repression in the name of intellectual honesty. Since the educated man believes that his beliefs should accord with the evidence—i.e., that his assent should attend the evidence—he may appear, in giving up his transcendent beliefs, to be abandoning his transcendent hopes as well. But I have already argued that such objects as life after death and God's existence—do meet the tests for justifiable hope—and are, therefore, entirely appropriate objects of hope—despite the fact that they may not also be appropriate objects of belief.

Bloch maintains that the greatest gift of Christianity was to introduce the "principle of hope" into the world. He says that Christianity insisted that one see the world and the future as it *could* become. However, the insight was frequently—notably, lost after the reign of Constantine, when the

Church ceased to be the revolutionary force it was and became instead the tool of the entrenched powers. Bloch believes that secular developments arising out of Christianity—Marxism, for instance, preserve the revolutionary insight. In fact, for Bloch, Marxism provides an ideology through which, precisely our transcendent hopes are best expressed. "Non-illusory" transcendent hopes are realizable, says Bloch, when we understand the Marxist principle of the socialistic transformation of the world.[81] "The dreams of a better life have always asked for a happiness that only Marxism can offer."[82] The inevitable development of the society or class of which one is a member is a "remedy against death."[83] Although the individual dies, one can, according to Marxist ideology, be assured that the march of history and the progress of society goes on.

Bloch has demonstrated in a convincing way, I believe, how many Christian hopes for the Kingdom of God and the New Age are embodied in Marxism. It's appeal lies in its promise to fulfill the basic hopes and aspirations of mankind. I also believe, however, that Bloch is in error in maintaining that the Marxist ideology provides a "remedy against death." If one's hope is that there exists a moral order in the universe in which justice triumphs and the highest good prevails (i.e., a condition of good in which the happiness of *each* individual is commensurate with his virtue), the Marxist assurance that we are moving toward a classless society will hardly suffice. It fails to take into account the moral sensitivity concerning *each* individual's worth—as embodied, for instance, in Kant's hope. (Cf. "Life After Death.")

Summary

In opposition to Camus' claim, it seems reasonable to hold (with Bloch) that modern man continues to harbor transcendent hopes. Applying the criterion of justifiable hopes, however, established earlier, we see that we need not accept Bloch's conclusion that the hopes of traditional religion—

personal survival, for instance—are merely "illusory." Nor, avoiding "sickly" attributions, need we admit Nietzsche's charge that our ultimate hopes are best pursued if God were "dead."

We have also pointed out difficulties inherent in Schopenhauer's and Freud's counsels of resignation. In particular, we have demonstrated that science as well as religion requires a foundation of hope. One cannot make discoveries if the fear of error and disappointment restricts our efforts within the protective cover of established theory. (Of course, the testing and confirmation of belief depends on the evidence.) At their creative edge, both science and religion are ventures in uncharted waters.

Let us turn, then, to James' defense of risk-taking.

James' Appeal to Give the Heart Its Chance

The rational man wants to believe true propositions and to disbelieve false ones. But religiously significant propositions never come with their truth-values printed on their sleeves.[84] The controlled testing possible in the natural sciences is never available and can never be adapted to the issues of ultimate religious concern. How, then, may one rationally decide which religious option to adopt?

As William James sees it, there are two distinct maxims to follow. On the one hand, (A) One must believe what is true; and on the other, (B) one must disbelieve what is false. James contends that the critical move is to decide to which maxim to give priority. "We may regard the chase for truth as paramount, and the avoidance of error as secondary; or we may, on the other hand, treat the avoidance of error as more imperative, and let truth take its chances."[85] Freud ranks (B) above (A), whereas Kant and James rank (A) above (B).

James is certainly correct that "Believe truth!" and "Shun error!" are "two materially different" maxims. Our criterion of justified belief, namely, that one must *believe* only those propositions for which one has adequate evidence, specifically concerns how to avoid error. There are, however, many true propositions for which one cannot obtain adequate evidence. If, further, one must disbelieve, or sceptically suspend judgment on, all propositions for which one does not have adequate evidence, then one has also de-emphasized, if not utterly devalued, maxim (A). By contrast, James advocates acting to minimize the risk of losing the truth—at least in cases where it much matters and where the evidence is not likely to be at hand—rather than acting to minimize the risk of falling into error. A very common objection to James holds that, in his enthusiasm for (A), he de-emphasizes and even disregards at times the maxim to avoid error.

Since believing truth and disbelieving falsehood are both desirable, what we should want is to be in the best possible position for both. The difficulty is to find a course which does not favor one at the expense of the other. Let us consider whether adopting the criterion of justified belief together with the criterion for justified hope (developed in the preceding chapter) provides such a middle course. If James' view runs the risk of leading us to believe falsehoods, *taken by itself*, the criterion of justified belief risks denying what is true.

The familiar appeal to suspend judgment, or to disbelieve *p*, in all cases in which one lacks sufficient evidence for (a justified) belief that *p* is an appeal to follow the maxim of equal assent to equal evidence. Often, however, in suspending our judgment concerning the truth of *p* we are *logically* bound (so it is supposed) that to act as if *p* were not the case. In fact, it often has that practical result. For example, the recommendation to suspend judgment in religious matters is often an appeal not merely to refrain from belief in these matters but to refrain as well from actual religious practices and commitment. One who follows the maxim (as it is usually understood) will, in critical situations, then be inclined to act as if the proposition in question were not true. That is, he will be inclined to act in an irreligious way.[86]

James offers the following rather acute description and criticism of this view:

Scepticism . . . is not avoidance of option, it is option of a certain particular kind of risk. *Better risk loss of truth than chance of error*, —that is your faith-vetoer's exact position. . . . To preach scepticism to us as a duty until "sufficient evidence" for religion be found, is tantamount therefore to telling us, when in presence of the religious hypothesis, that to yield to our fear of its being error is wiser and better than to yield to our hope that it may be true. [87]

A similar point is made in "The Sentiment of Rationality":

If I refuse to bail out a boat because I am in doubt whether my effort will keep her afloat, I am really helping to sink her. . . . He who commands himself not to be credulous of God, of duty, of freedom, of immortality, may again and again be indistinguishable from him who dogmatically denies them.[88]

Believing, disbelieving, being sceptical, hoping, fearing, being indifferent, etc. entail (given normal conditions) certain sorts of "action"—"action" includes, here, refraining from action, and certain sorts of action form criteria for ascribing such predicates to particular persons. But, just as hoping that p and believing that p may involve similar actions, so, too disbelieving that p and being sceptical that p, or even completely suspending judgment about p may result in similar actions. For example, whereas both the belief and the hope that God exists are likely to result, say, in "taking holy water and having masses said,"[89] so, too, disbelieving that God exists or skeptically suspending judgment about God's existence are likely to result, say, in failing to darken the door of a church (unless, of course the person in question were an American politician).

In effect, then the skeptical position (this is not intended to cover all forms of skepticism) results in one's acting as if not-p in just those cases in which one lacks sufficient evidence for a justified belief in p. A premise required by the skeptic's move is this: that belief that p be a *necessary* condition for rationally performing any action considered appropriate if p were known to be true. However, as we have already argued, belief that p is *not* always (as in the cases of interest here) a necessary (or, for that matter, a sufficient) condition for rationally performing actions that would be appropriate if p were known to be true. In the cases in question, it would be sufficient that one merely hope that p (without actually believing that p).

James appears[90] to accept the erroneous principle underlying the skeptics move, of the relation between belief and action, although he uses the principle, of course to obtain a different conclusion altogether. He appears to hold that if one does not believe that p, he will not be able to act as if p were true, or to perform actions appropriate to bringing p about. Hence, in cases—as in matters regarding God's existence—that cannot be strictly decided on evidential grounds, James maintains that one has the right to choose (i.e., to believe) the side one favors. For example, if one favors the option that God exists, one has the right to *believe* that God exists. In fact, it would be irrational to favor the thesis that goes against one's wants. "Our passional nature not only lawfully may, but must, decide an option between propositions, whenever it is a genuine option that cannot by its nature be decided on intellectual grounds. . . ."[91]

Even if one concedes that belief is not a necessary condition for performing an action appropriately as a rational agent and even if one does not concede James' claims regarding justified beliefs (incompatible, of course, with our strong Lockean criterion), one may still share James' criticisms of scepticism and maintain a view regarding religious commitment not altogether unlike his. If one hopes, without believing that what is desirable (p) obtains, one may still (rationally) perform those actions he would perform if he believed that p. In hoping that p, one fixes on the positive possibility that p is true. One makes use of this as the rational basis for his action, cognizant that he has no evidence for the actual truth of p. He realizes, therefore, that he must take a cognitive risk. But in doing that he is not violating the maxim to avoid error (despite James' thesis, on the interpretation given).

From this point of view (combining the criterion of justified belief with that of justified hope), the alternative that requires that when we have little or no evidence, we suspend cognitive judgment regarding, or suspect, or doubt, or strongly presume against the propositions in question—in spite of a strong desire that they be true, though transcendent —is a much too restrictive policy. James very aptly describes the rejected thesis:

> We have no right, this doctrine tells us, to dream dreams, or suppose anything about the unseen part of the universe, merely because to do so may be for what we are pleased to call our highest interests.[92]

If our argument is sound, then James' reaction is well-founded.

> When I look at the religious question as it really puts itself to concrete man, and when I think of all the possibilities which both practically and theoretically it involves, then this command that we shall put a stopper on our heart, instincts, and courage, and wait— acting of course meanwhile more or less as if religion were *not* true— till doomsday, or till such times as our intellect and sense working together may have raked in evidence enough,—this command, I say, seems to me the queerest idol ever manufactured in the philosophic cave.[93]

James' sentiment is the very same that motivates the move to combine the criterion for justified hope with the (strong) criterion for justified belief. It is the attempt to adhere equally to both maxims. The criterion of hope helps us to seek the truth (in contexts of personal concern, in which such concerns are *morally* justifiable—cf. the conditions for justified hope).[94] The criterion of justified belief helps us to shun error. To adopt James' sentiment, rejecting his thesis regarding justified belief, is, then, to come very close to the position I wish to defend. In "The Will to Believe" James means to provide "a defense of our right to adopt a *believing attitude* in religious matters, in spite of the fact that our mere logical intellect may not have been coerced."[95] Now, a believing attitude toward p may signify either believing that p or merely being favorably disposed toward believing that p (without actually doing so). The latter option is, clearly, the relevant one. Having a believing attitude, therefore, is a weaker notion than having a belief. If one hopes that p, without actually believing that p, it will still be true of him that he is favorably disposed toward belief that p. Hence, one who hopes that p takes a believing attitude toward p.

James views his effort as an attempt to justify *faith*. His notion of faith is actually quite close to our own account of hope (developed in the chapter on the phenomenology of hope).

> Faith means belief in something concerning which doubt is still theoretically possible; and as the test of belief is willingness to act, one may say that faith is the readiness to act in a cause the prosperous issue of which is not certified to us in advance.[96]

As we have seen, the hope that p entails the disposition or readiness to act in order to bring p about, even when the odds are clearly against p. P, of course, is, relevantly, the object of our desire.

James goes on to say that certainty that p, or a guarantee that p, is not required.

> All that the human heart wants is its chance. It will willingly forego certainty in universal matters if only it can be allowed to feel that in them it has that same inalienable right to run risks, which no one dreams of refusing to it in the pettiest practical affairs.[97]

He is willing, therefore, to settle for rather less than the faith some believers require. Certainty that p is a more stringent constraint than belief that p. But even the belief that p is not required, on James' view, if the notion of believing that p entails expecting that p is the case. What he wishes to justify includes cognizance of the risk of possible disappointment and the willingness to take that risk; and that is tantamount to hope.

James opposes a view which he believes would (in the name of reason) enslave our spirits, our desires, our hearts. It is not that he opposes reasons and evidence. But he argues that it is hardly reasonable to use reason in order to frustrate the human heart, by commanding it to *follow*, or wait upon the facts. In matters of the heart, he holds "possibilities, not finished facts,are the realities with which we have actively to deal."[98] In fact, he claims enthusiastically that we have a right to *believe* (at our own risk) any hypothesis live enough to tempt our will.[99] The familiar complaint that he is being far too liberal here is not without merit. For James' remarks make it appear that he condones all forms of self-deception and wishful thinking. But he also makes his point more clearly and less sweepingly—as in the essay, "Is Life Worth Living?" There, he says, ". . .we are free to trust at our own risks anything that is not impossible, and that can bring analogies to bear in its behalf."[100]

Consider, for example, the proposition that God exists—i.e. that there exists a cosmic power which advances whatever is creative, just, and benevolent. We cannot collect sufficient evidence for its truth, but it may be true all the same. Also we *can* bring to bear in its behalf analogies like the following:

> Our dogs . . . are in our human life but not of it. They witness hourly the outward body of events whose inner meaning cannot, by any possible operation, be revealed to their intelligence,—events in which they themselves often play the cardinal part. My terrier bites a teasing boy, for example, and the father demands damages. The dog may be present at every step of the negotiations, and see the money paid, without an inkling of what it all means, without a suspicion that it has anything to do with *him*; and he never *can* know in his natural dog's life.[101]

In short, we may be in our dogs' position, regarding God's existence. So the theist need not be dealing with inconceivable possibilities. He is, of course, restricted to his native ignorance.

James says that, in such cases, we have the right "to trust at our own risk." But in order to risk one must understand that he is risking; one must realize that he lacks supporting evidence for the proposition he favors. What, then, does it mean to *trust*? Apparently it means to risk oneself on the possibility of truth, acting as if the proposition were actually true. James says:

> And to trust our religious demands means first of all to live in the light of them, and to act as if the invisible world which they suggest were real. It is a fact of human nature, that men can live and die by the help of a sort of faith that goes without a single dogma or definition.[102]

In this situation, to trust appears to be to hope.

Instead of seeing James' task as the attempt to justify the belief that *p*, we may, then, reasonably reinterpret his remarks as the attempt to justify the hope that *p*. Hence, even if we concede to his critics the principle that belief or assent to a proposition ought to be proportional to the evidence in its favor, we may still vindicate James' "believing attitude." The justification of the hope that *p* is not so much a function of the strength of the evidence favoring *p* as it is of the strength of, and the grounds for, the desire that *p*—assuming that *p* is possible and that all necessary background beliefs are justified. Even if we have no non-arbitrary way to assess the evidential odds—as with propositions like "God exists" or "There is an afterlife"—the strength of our desire that such propositions be true, and the moral and pragmatic grounds supporting such desires make it quite rational to hope that they be true. Wishful thinking is not the issue. What is condoned, rather, is taking risks in the name of truth, where truth cannot possibly be gained without such a risk. Hence, the heart is given its chance without denying reason its say.

The great Russian Jewish author, Lev Shestov—a philosopher little known in England and America, but recognized Continentally as one of the founders of existentialism—offers the following effective contrast between the views of the critics of hope and of the theologian of hope:

> When God says to Abraham, "Leave your country, your friends and your father's house, and go to the land that I will show you," Abraham obeys and "leaves without knowing where he is going."

. . . All this is according to the Bible. But common sense judges quite otherwise. He who goes without knowing where he is going is a weak and frivolous man, and a faith which is founded on nothing (now faith is always founded on nothing, for it is faith itself that wishes to "found") cannot be in any way "imputed for righteousness." The same conviction, clearly and neatly formulated and raised to the level of method, reigns in science, which was born of common sense. Science, in fact, is science only so long as it does not admit faith and always demands of man that he realize what he is doing and know where he is going. Scientific philosophy, or to put it another way, the philosophy which utilizes in its search for its truths the same methods that science employs in its search for its truths also wishes to know where it is going and where it is leading its adherents. It follows from this that faith is distinguished from science, above everything else, by its methods.

The believer goes forward, without looking to the right or to the left, without asking where he is going, without calculating. The scientist will not take a step without looking around him, without asking, and is afraid to budge from his place. He wishes to know beforehand where he will arrive. Which of these two methods leads us to "truth?" One can discuss this matter, but it is beyond doubt that he alone will be able to attain the promised land who, like Abraham, decides to go forward without knowing where he is going. And if philosophy wishes to attain the promised land. . . . It must . . . teach men at all events to go forward without calculating, without seeing anything beforehand, without even knowing where they are going.[103]

We ourselves have been trying to *combine* Shestov's insight with a rather rigorous criterion of justified belief (favored by common sense and science). Shestov was not interested in reconciliation. In fact, his own thesis, in *Athens and Jerusalem*, maintains that the religious and scientific views are quite incompatible. We oppose him, therefore, on the grounds that both may be benefited. In combining the principles of justified belief and justified hope, we are advocating a moderate, common sense rational basis for religious commitment itself.

We have, then, attempted to establish that one may be rationally justified in adopting the fundamental tenets of traditional theistic religion to guide one's life. The rational moral agent wants a world in which what is morally most desirable—the highest good—obtains. Hence, he wants a world in which God exists and men's souls are immortal. Furthermore, God's existence and personal survival are possible. And analogical arguments may be mustered in their behalf. Hence, not only has one a right to hope that God exists and that there is a future life; to do so is to act the part of a reasonable moral agent. For such hopes are justified and firm against objection.

5 The Venture of Religion

If the argument offered is successful so far, then such basic religious *hopes* as the hope that God exists and that there is an after life are justifiable—even if the counterpart *beliefs* are not, for lack of sufficient evidence. The question remains, whether the resultant position is *religiously adequate.* Obviously, many believers have not confined themselves within the limits of religious commitment here advanced. I shall argue, however, that this view not only meets comparatively stringent epistemological requirements, but is religiously attractive as well. What is relinquished in terms of hope is far less important, religiously, than what is gained.

We shall begin by examining some arguments offered by Gabriel Marcel and Søren Kierkegaard in which they claim that it is actually religiously advantageous that we lack objective evidence for our religious beliefs. For, they say, religious faith or commitment requires risking or venturing in a way that is possible only in the face of objective uncertainty and doubt regarding the appropriate objects; that is, in short, if one lives in hope, not in knowledge or belief. We shall then go on to inquire about the role that evidence and belief about basic religious propositions do, and must, play in religious affirmation. I shall argue that the "logic" of religious-belief is more similar to that of HOPE than to that of ordinary belief. For example, I shall try to show that the seeming plausibility of recent non-cognitive analyses of religious language may be bettered by construing religious-belief in terms of hope. The parallel between religious-belief and hope, with respect to truth and evidence, is rather compelling. I shall not, however, argue that the language of ordinary religious belief is simply the language of hope. I maintain, rather, that there is a strong similarity between the two, and that the analysis of hope illuminates the logic of religious belief. Finally (in the last chapter), I shall examine some of the differences between the two. There, the epistemic and religious superiority of a commitment based on hope rather than belief will be demonstrated.

Marcel and Kierkegaard: The Religious Life as a Venture in Uncertainty

Marcel and Kierkegaard rather boldly—almost shockingly— maintain that it is a good thing we lack theoretical grounds for believing that God exists, or that there is a life after death. It is certainly not something to lament. For if we had supporting evidence, religious-belief would not even be possible. Therefore, *from the religious point of view*, it is good that we cannot rationally support the assertion that God exists. If those who have sought to prove that God exists, or that men's souls are immortal, had actually been successful, they would, by their success, have destroyed the possibility of religious belief. A lack of objective evidence is, then, a necessary condition of religious faith.

Even if objective knowledge of religious truths could be obtained, it would not, Marcel holds, yield the desired result.[1] For then, what would normally have been considered an affirmation of religious faith would (if the metaphysics of optimism made good its claims) prove to be no more than a statement of science.

> Supposing that we could demonstrate objectively, that is to say in a valid way, a way valid for all thought in general, that our universe is governed by a spiritual principle, the demonstration would render impossible the radical freedom that can only manifest itself by faith. Faith (and thence spirituality) is only possible if metaphysical doubt

is in some way imposed on the mind by the nature—in itself in-determinable—of the object. Were a science of providence possible, providence would cease to be a religious affirmation.[2]

So a lack of objective evidence is positively required in order to have a *religious* faith. Marcel likens adopting an attitude of faith to "opening a credit."[3] The creditor may always fail to live up to his agreement (cf. Chapter 2, above); one's religious hopes are always risked. Inevitably, religious faith "is a jump, a bet—and, like all bets, it can be lost."[4] Because of this, Marcel claims that the emotions involved in hope (already discussed) are essential features of a religious faith. As we have also seen, the calculation of the probability that p plays but a minor role in the formation of the relevant hopes.[5]

Marcel believes that religious faith, like the special range of hopes we have considered, has the greatest chance of thriving in a tragic context—in which loyalty to one's personal values and commitments (as to one's wife, or to being a moral person) require accepting a radical cognitive risk. One's sense of loyalty to values expressed in p, *rather than* belief that p is probable, must, if one's commitment to p is to be religiously significant, count as one's motivation. To base one's com-mitment primarily on probabilistic beliefs would be a cheap and shallow way incommensurate with a genuine religious engagement.

We must pause to notice that there is some ambiguity here. It is not entirely clear whether Marcel's is a logical thesis, or whether it is a normative one. That is, his claim might be that it is a necessary feature of *religious* commitment to p that one be relevantly motivated by something other than one's belief that p; for p must remain in essential doubt. Absent that condition, the commitment cannot be a religious one. Or, his claim might be that a religious commitment to p can-not be commendable if one's belief that p is probable is a (primary) reason for being committed to p. The latter claim —the normative one—appears to be the only plausible alter-native of the two. Taken normatively, however, it still remains ambiguous. It might be the claim merely that intellectual honesty entails that one recognize in one's heart that one's commitment is not based on objective knowledge. That is, honesty might require that one concede one's faith to be based on hope rather than belief; hence, that a religion based on hope is superior to one based on belief. But Marcel (also, Kierkegaard) wishes to hold instead that a religious commitment construed reflexively as not supported by objective evidence at all is superior to one that is (or is claimed to be) supported by favorable evidence. Kierkegaard makes very much the same claim. In the *Concluding Unscientific Postscript,* he says:

> While faith has hitherto had a profitable schoolmaster in the existing uncertainty, it would have in the new certainty its most dangerous enemy. For if passion is eliminated, faith no longer exists, and certainty and passion do not go together.[6]

He also says, later, "it is precisely a misunderstanding to seek an objective assurance, thereby avoiding the risk in which passion chooses and continues to live, reaffirming its choice."[7] And he presents us with the following dilemma:

> Suppose a man who wishes to acquire faith; let the comedy begin. He wishes to have faith, but he wishes also to safeguard himself by means of an objective inquiry and its approximation-process. What happens? With the help of the approximation-process the absurd becomes something different, it becomes probable, it becomes increasingly probable, it becomes extremely and emphatically probable. Now he is ready to believe it, and he ventures to claim for himself that he does not believe as shoemakers and tailors and simple folk believe, but only after long deliberation. Now he is ready to believe it; and lo, now it has become precisely impossible to believe it. Anything that is almost probable, or probable, or extremely and emphatically probable, is something he can almost know, or as good as know, or extremely and emphatically almost *know*—but it is impossible to *believe.*[8]

For Kierkegaard, then, the necessary conditions of genuine

religious-belief include passionate commitment, intensity of feeling, the willingness to take risks and make sacrifices. In fact, he insists that "it must be strenuous in the highest degree so to believe."[9]

Kierkegaard contrasts two forms of religiousness in terms of their cognitive differences. One (religiousness B) depends on the Christ-event, the Absolute Paradox. This uniquely Christian form of religiousness we shall examine later. The other (religiousness A) is based on Socratic ignorance and is motivated by hope—by the passion for the possible. According to Kierkegaard, Socrates—distinguished from Plato, in that he offered no proofs for immortality, did not know whether men's souls were immortal. He had no evidence. But, says Kierkegaard:

> On this "if" he risks his entire life, he has the courage to meet death, and he has with the passion of the infinite so determined the pattern of his life that it must be found acceptable—if there is an immortality. . . . The bit of uncertainty that Socrates had, helped him because he himself contributed the passion of the infinite. . . . A young girl may enjoy all the sweetness of love on the basis of what is merely a weak hope that she is beloved, because she rests everything on this weak hope.[10]

Kierkegaard holds, then, that it is a necessary condition of vital religious faith that one be willing to take such risks. "Without risk faith is an impossibility. . . . To believe, to wish to believe, is to change one's life into a trial; daily test is the trial of faith."[11] Without the risk of uncertainty, the passion, the enthusiasm, the commitment—the essential elements of religious faith—will be lacking. Conversely, if the passion and commitment are present, certainty is not needed. Objective uncertainty, therefore, works to the benefit of religious faith.

Kierkegaard maintains:

> I contemplate the order of nature in the hope of finding God, and I see omnipotence and wisdom; but I also see much else that disturbs

> my mind and excites anxiety. The sum of all this is an objective un-
> certainty. But it is for this very reason that the inwardness becomes
> as intense as it is, for it embraces this objective uncertainty with the
> entire passion of the infinite.[12]

The intensity of "inwardness," which is an essential feature of the religious stance, is, according to Kierkegaard, inversely related to the objective certainty of the object of one's religious attention. "The more objective security the less inwardness (for inwardness is precisely subjectivity), and the less objective security the more profound the possible inwardness."[13] Objective certainty, then, is inimical to religious faith. Kierkegaard says:

> If I take the uncertainty away—in order to get a still greater certain-
> ty—then I do not get a believer in his humility, in fear and trembling,
> but I get an aesthetic coxcomb, a devil of a fellow, who wishes,
> speaking loosely, to fraternize with God.[14]

Kierkegaard thinks of the religious attitude as one of continual suffering and striving,[15] a seeking after certainty without ever attaining it.[16] He refers to the "awakened" person—that is, the one who "knows himself to be absolutely secure in his own God-relationship"[17]—and claims that such a person has merely strayed into the religious sphere. He lacks commitment and depth, and simply uses his (supposed) objective certainty regarding God to escape the tension and struggle of the truly religious life; actually, according to Kierkegaard, he behaves thus in order to live in aesthetic complacency. For *some* cases at least, the analysis and the criticism seem entirely correct.

Kierkegaard's thesis, however, requires that the inverse relationship between inwardness and objective certainty obtain in *all* cases bearing on claims of certainty regarding one's relationship to God. Could Kierkegaard have estab-lished such a correlation?

It is a psychological fact that one needs much less of a commitment to pursue a goal, *g*, if he thinks *g* is nearly certain to be attained than if he thinks *g* is decidedly uncertain. On the other hand, one *could* be just as committed to pursuing g if g were nearly certain of being attained as when g is thought to be uncertain. For example, S, who expects C to win an election, could be just as committed to C's campaign (could work diligently for C, vote for C, be happy if C wins, etc.) as T, who, though he very much wants C to win, thinks C's victory very unlikely. Of course, S might easily become complacent and slacken his pace, but he need not. On the other hand, T is more in danger of despairing than S. But again T's commitment to C's victory need not weaken. So, if, by inwardness, Kierkegaard simply means commitment, the inverse relationship between inwardness and certainty would not obtain.

But that is not Kierkegaard's position. Inwardness is not mere commitment. It also includes *intensity* of feeling and a sense of inner *tension*.[18] As we have just seen, commitment to g is not inversely proportional to objective certainty. But certainty that g would resolve the relevant tensions of anxiety and doubt and perplexity. With objective certainty, then, comes a feeling of ease, peace, (rest relative to g).[19] On this view, Kierkegaard would probably agree with the following phenomenological description by James:

> Any perfectly fluent course of thought awakens but little feeling; but when the movement is inhibited, or when the thought meets with difficulties, we experience distress. It is only when the distress is upon us that we can be said to strive, to crave, or to aspire. When enjoying plenary freedom either in the way of motion or of thought, we are in a sort of anaesthetic state in which we might say with Walt Whitman, if we cared to say anything about ourselves at such times, "I am sufficient as I am."[20]

One who considers g to be objectively certain encounters no obstacles. Reflecting on g, he has a feeling of the sufficiency of the present moment. He is at ease. In Kierkegaard's terminology, he is an aesthete.

But then, if one takes it to be objectively certain, g cannot, on Kierkegaard's account, be an object of religious regard. If it is to be such, then commitment to g must involve a risk and must involve its concomitant emotions.

> Here is the task of the religious address. Were it merely to say the brief word: "Venture everything," there would not be needed more than one speaker in an entire kingdom, while the longest discourse must not forget the venture.[21]

Ethico-religious existence is "an enthusiastic venture in uncertainty."[22] To venture is itself to undertake a long and toilsome journey *without knowing* whether the enterprise will succeed.[23]

> Strange to say, the wisdom that concerns this or that in life is not so very rare, and one may not infrequently see an existing individual who expresses existentially a relationship to a relative end, testifying to the fact that he has planned his life with this end in view. That he has given up whatever might prove to be an obstacle, and sets his hope upon what is to be gained by so doing. But an existing individual who expresses existentially a relationship to the absolute good is perhaps a rare exception. Such a one could say with truth: "I exist in such and such a manner, I have made such and such sacrifices in transforming my existence, so that if I hoped for this life alone, I should be the most wretched of all creatures, that is, the most terribly deceived, self-deceived in refusing to grasp what lay to my hand."[24]

If (as I do) one believes that, in its highest form, the religious life is just this sort of venture—a venture offering a context for the greatest possible risk, intensity of feeling, demonstration of passionate commitment—then one will agree with Kierkegaard that the object of religious commitment cannot be certain of attainment. Surely, the imagery of some sort of venture plays a prominent role in religious literature (cf. in St. Paul, Miguel de Unamuno, Paul Tillich), though it must be admitted that the venture acknowledged often is not as venturesome as Kierkegaard requires. James usefully documents the fact that many who are "deeply religious" are apparently willing to make great sacrifices and to risk everything in the name of their commitment.[25] They are more accurately described in terms of risking and striving than in terms of security and ease. On the argument, one who lives religiously must live in hope rather than in knowledge. But if Kierkegaard is right about the venture and right about the import of certainty, then whoever describes the religious commitment in terms of venture imagery and also holds that the religious objective is certain of attainment is making a straightforward logical mistake. He is conjoining contradictory notions: one cannot consistently have both the certainty and the venture.

Which alternative should be favored? Should one opt for (A) the vision of religious life as an uncertain venture requiring unrequited striving, courage, personal resolve against all odds; or (B) the vision of cosmic security with its attendant sense of well-being, world order, tranquility? Perhaps it is empirically true—as Kierkegaard, Schopenhauer, Freud, and Camus believed—that the majority of religious believers have wanted their religion to insure a sense of cosmic security rather than to serve as a venture (as in Kierkegaard's strenuous sense). But this cannot be an issue that can be properly settled by majority preference. If the tranquility and cosmic security required could be gained without conceptual cheating, without violating reasonable cognitive constraints, without losing the passionate commitment of a genuinely religious life, without inconsistency, then, very probably, it ought to be preferred. But, as I shall finally argue, the (B) alternative cannot surmount these difficulties. It remains an ideal toward which one may be drawn rather than a confirmed condition within which one may confidently live.

Religious-belief as Hope: Wittgensteinian Reflections

Doubtless, the cosmic security view we have ascribed to the ordinary believer is a caricature. But it does not differ from this view as one might think. If we examine the "logic" of the ordinary religious-believer's (religious) assertions, we find that the belief-that certain entities exist, or that certain events have occurred or will occur, does not play the crucial role it is often thought to play. I shall, in fact, argue that the ordinary believer can accept as adequate an account of religious faith in which, for instance, the *belief-that* God exists, or that Christ was raised from the dead about 37 A.D., or that the Last Judgment will occur plays no role at all. The hope that such things obtain may be sufficient for a religious commitment. It is their possibility rather than their actuality that the believer needs to confirm in order to sustain a vital religious life. If so, then we have resolved a difficult epistemoligical problem. The task of justifying one's religious faith then becomes quite manageable. (It would not be, of course, if it rested on assertions about Christ's resurrection, or the last judgment.)

Let us consider, now, an actual religious position based on hope rather than on belief, and then construct the argument for its full defense.

Miguel de Unamuno, one of the great religious thinkers of the early twentieth century, affirms that a living faith and a realistic theology must be based on hope alone. He says: ". . . we do not hope because we believe, but rather we believe because we hope. It is hope in God, it is the ardent longing that there may be a God who guarantees the eternity of consciousness, that leads us to believe in Him."[26] The starting point is hope, not belief. On the basis of hope, one comes to belief-in God. "What is certain is that for thinking believers today, faith is, before all and above all, wishing that God may exist."[27] Here, "wishing" is clearly synonymous with "hoping."

Unamuno takes the paradoxical remark of the father of the demoniac, in the *Gospel according to St. Mark* (9:24)— "Lord, I believe; help thou mine unbelief!"—to be the paradigm of modern-day faith. The seeming contradiction

> gives to the heart's cry of the father of the demoniac its most profound human value. His faith is a faith based upon incertitude. Because he believes—that is to say, because he wishes to believe, because he has need that his son should be cured—he beseeches the Lord to help his unbelief, his doubt that such a cure could be effected.[28]

The faith which Unamuno describes (and adheres to) is not one of peace and security but rather of suffering and struggling amid uncertainty and nagging doubts. Faith is quixotic. Unamuno saw himself, in fact, as a modern-day Quixote. There is even a close parallel between Unamuno's reference to Quixote and Kierkegaard's account of the "Knight of Faith," in *Fear and Trembling.*[29] Unamuno correctly stresses the aspect of venture. But he also suggests the merely *imaginary* character of the object for which one ventures, which is hardly a necessary feature of the religious position. Unamuno cannot be said to have developed a coherent theology of hope. He was, in fact, neither a systematic nor a consistent thinker. But even from this brief account, we may begin to draw out the themes and implications of a theology of hope.

In some lectures printed under the title, *Lectures and Conversations on Aesthetics, Psychology and Religious Belief,* Ludwig Wittgenstein provides a basis for the required argument.[30] Wittgenstein speculates:

> Suppose someone were a believer and said: "I believe in a Last Judgment," and I said: "Well, I'm not so sure. Possibly." You would say that there is an enormous gulf between us. If he said "There is a German aeroplane overhead," and I said "Possibly, I'm not so sure," you'd say we were fairly near.[31]

Why is there a gulf in the first case and not in the second?

The issue is not one of disagreement respecting evidence for p (e.g., p = the Last Judgment). For instance, R a religious person, might believe that the evidence for p was not very well established. Yet p might be "the firmest of all beliefs [for R], because the man risks things on account of it which he would not do on things which are by far better established for him."[32] S, another believer, might, on the other hand, believe that the evidence was in favor of the coming of Judgment Day—say, S believed that he was clairvoyant. Still, Wittgenstein (rightly) claims, the "belief in this happening wouldn't be at all a religious belief."[33]

Wittgenstein's suggestion is that the wide gulf between religious and non-religious persons misleadingly appears to be based on a disagreement about evidence, but is actually a disagreement about how one is to live one's life.

> Suppose somebody made this guidance for his life: believing in the Last Judgment. Whenever he does anything, this is before his mind. In a way, how are we to know whether to say he believes this will happen or not?[34]

The religious person (in our instance) lives with a picture of the Last Judgment before his mind. In some sense, the non-religious person lives without that picture.[35] Might this not account for the enormous gulf between them?

Some apologists for religious-belief have felt obliged to concede that, if the objective basis for the objects of one's devotion were tangential to religious commitment, the ordinary religious believer could not be said to be a rational person. But since a believer ought to be rational, the apologist continues, the defense of religion requires that we demonstrate that religious-beliefs are actually well founded.

Clearly, if he accepts the strong criterion of justified belief, the apologist is assuming a very large burden. To be successful, he must show that beliefs such as "God exists," "There will be a Last Judgment," "Christ rose from the grave about 37 A.D." have an extremely high probability of being true. High probability is required since the religious believer's assent to such propositions is so complete. Fortunately, if our account of religious-belief, or of faith as hope, is correct, all such apologetic attempts are misguided. For it now appears that religious-beliefs are acquired, and may be evaluated and interpreted, in ways quite different from those that involve (most) other beliefs. We may mark the contrast conveniently by hyphenating (as I have) "religious-belief."[36] Wittgenstein remarks:

> There is this extraordinary use of the word 'believe.' One talks of believing and at the same time one doesn't use 'believe' as one does ordinarily. You might say (in the normal use): "You only believe— oh well. . . ." Here it is used entirely differently; on the other hand it is not used as we generally use the word 'know.'[37]

Ordinarily, the claim either to believe or to know that p imposes on one a burden of evidence. When I say that I know that p, I signify that I can cite evidence for p—possibly even of a very rigorous sort. Usually, however, the religious person does not claim to have supporting evidence when he asserts, for example, "I believe in life after death" or, "I believe in the Last Judgment (that is, that ultimately justice, love, and beauty will win out)." If he offers grounds for his assertion, most likely he will offer reasons to explain the source of his belief or his motivation for believing; or, if he appears to offer support for the truth of his claim, the reasons will be *untestable* ones—for instance, that he heard the voice of God, or that the Bible conveys God's word or that he had a revelation.

Detractors of religion have been quick to point out that revelations and visions, as well as less dramatic religious experiences, are hardly good evidence and would hardly stand up in other domains of inquiry. Apologists have answered by trying to show that the evidence is not as weak as it appears to be. But if a religious assertion is essentially an expression of what one takes as guidance for one's life, then both the detractors and the apologists are misguided. Detractors take the religious person to be arguing that his beliefs can actually meet the testing requirements of the empirical sciences; and apologists try to demonstrate that his claims are scientifically respectable. Wittgenstein offers the following criticism:

> If you compare it with anything in Science which we call evidence, you can't credit that anyone could soberly argue: "Well, I had this dream . . . therefore . . . Last Judgment." You might say: "For a blunder, that's too big." If you suddenly wrote numbers down on the blackboard, and then said: "Now, I'm going to add," and then said: "2 and 21 is 13," etc., I'd say: "This is no blunder."[38]

In effect, what he says is that if we are to understand the religious commitment, we must see that in claiming to believe in the Last Judgment, one is doing something quite different from what he would be doing if he said he believed there was an airplane over there. He is at least affirming that he is committing himself to a certain way of life. He is saying (in part) that the norm by which he lives entails viewing his own actions and those of other men through the eyes of the divine Judge. It is true that a certain dream, or vision, or even the experience of terror may be religiously relevant. For example, it may impel one to construct a sense of the meaning or unity of one's life which one might otherwise be without. If we understood one's reference to a particular vision or a particular para-normal experience as part of the explanation of why one has committed himself to a particular religious norm—why he views it as personally compelling rather than merely as evidence for the truth of the claim, "The Last Judgment will take place"—we should have a clearer grasp of the "logic" of religious assertion.

It seems, therefore, that it is more fruitful to compare the religious assertion, "I believe in life after death," with certain cases of "I hope that . . ." than with ordinary uses of "I believe that . . ." For, in expressions of hope of the relevant sort, as in expressions of religious devotion, one is speaking first and foremost about himself, his wants, his commitments, his values, etc. He is not making a forecast of any sort—with or without sufficient evidence. But this is not to say that if the object of his religious-belief were shown to be impossible, or unimaginable, the religious believer would not give up his religious-belief. Without a doubt, he would, as a rational agent, give it up as he would, hope.

If the various non-cognitivist analyses of religious language (widely discussed some years ago) were correct,[39] one would not be expected, on rational grounds, to give up his religious-belief if the object of his religious-belief proved non-existent. It does seem, however, that one would give up his religious-belief under such circumstances. That fact alone counts strongly against the non-cognitivist account. An analysis in terms of hope meets this difficulty, at the same time that it accommodates the very reasons which appear to favor the non-cognitivist analysis.

Quite naturally, the religious believer regards evidence

relative to p in the same way one would who is hopeful that p. He would appreciate more evidence, and he would not go contrary to decisive evidence. He would, in fact, give up his religious-belief, or hope, that p, if he discovered that p was impossible. A typical religious-believer may, objectively speaking, agree with critics that evidence for his religious-belief is rather poor. Still, he may feel that he is not obliged to give it up. He *would* normally give up his non-religious beliefs, if the evidence were sufficiently weak or unfavorable. This may seem to indicate that he must be reacting irrationally in the religious sphere. But, his response may actually be religiously and epistemically correct. In fact, his intuition that he ought to avoid the temptation to give up his religious-belief in such a situation conforms with what we should expect if religious-belief resembles hope more than ordinary belief.

An important dissimilarity between religious-belief and ordinary belief is this: good evidence is sufficient to establish a belief, but not to establish a religious-belief. Conceivably, there might be extremely good evidence for the hypothesis of life after death. Suppose, for example, after years of research, that hypothesis appeared to be better established than most other scientific hypotheses. The entire issue—the data and the experiments—might be made quite intelligible to the non-specialist public. One might, then, easily have enough grounds for believing the hypothesis. Still, that evidence would not provide sufficient basis for the religious-belief concerning life after death. There is, as we have seen, a logical gap between ordinary belief-that p and the total commitment which, as Kierkegaard and Wittgenstein have pointed out, is an essential element of religious-belief. Good evidence for p would not provide grounds for holding p in religious regard. Similarly, good evidence for p would not provide grounds for finding p desirable—hence, a possible object of hope.

The dissimilarity between the two kinds of belief may be seen if we compare the resultant attitude toward the loss of each sort of belief. Suppose, for example that a central belief about the physical world proves to be false. Imagine, for instance, that one were compelled by the relevant evidence to disbelieve that the earth is (approximately) spherical. He would be greatly surprised to lear that his previous belief was false. On the other hand, imagine that one feels compelled to abandon a central tenet of his religious-belief— for example, the belief that God exists.[40] There would not be surprise in abandoning a basic religious-belief as in giving up a basic scientific belief. The religious-believer is more likely to display disappointment, panic, disillusionment, a change of heart rather than mere surprise.

We expect one's reaction to be one of surprise when it turns out that a proposition he strongly believed to be true proves to be false and must be rejected. This is probably one of the marks of ordinary belief (cf. Chapter 3, above). If they were held in the way scientific beliefs are held, then, given the serious devotion with which they are normally held, we should expect even greater surprise on finding that a religious-belief must be rejected than a fundamental belief about the physical world. But the strength of beliefs in the two domains are measured on quite different scales. Whereas the strength of ordinary belief is largely a measure of one's expectation that p, the strength of religious-belief is for the most part, a measure of one's commitment, or one's devotion, to p. Hence—as with hope—we would expect deep disappointment on the part of the religious-believer, rather than mere surprise, if he is compelled to give up his belief in God.

If the "logic" of religious-belief closely resembles the logic of hope and is dissimilar to that of belief, ought we not expect the justification of hopes and religious-belief to be similar as well? The criterion of justified hope has already been considered. With appropriate adjustments, then, it should apply to religious-beliefs as well. The advantages of admitting justified hopes should apply to religious-beliefs as well.

To construe religious faith as falling within the range of hope rather than the range of belief does not, of course, preclude the possibility that *beliefs* that certain entities exist, or that certain events will occur, may constitute salient features of the religious venture of some. But it does show that a great deal of what is normally meant by religious affirmation can be easily expressed without appeal to beliefs, which, in any case—given our epistemological position—cannot possibly be justified. Hence, assuming the correctness of that position, more can be gained by construing religious-belief as hope than is lost by its adoption.

Religious-Belief as Hope: Logical Analyses

I should now like to consider what analysis we must give, consistent with the view of religious-belief offered, of two key religious propositions, namely, "I believe in a life after death," and "I believe in God."

Most people concerned about life after death typically speak of *believing in* life after death rather than of *believing that* there is life after death. Admittedly, the verbal shift is often of no philosophical interest. For instance, one often hears of someone's believing in the Loch Ness monster, or of an early scientist's belief in ether or phlogiston or celestial spheres. In these expressions, "belief in" simply signifies that a certain entity or phenomenon exists or occurs. If these served as our model, then "belief in life after death" would be synonymous with "belief that there is a life after death." There are, however, cases of "belief in" that behave quite differently. Assimilated to those, "belief in life after death" would not be synonymous with "belief that there is a life after death." In fact, on that model, "belief that there is a life after death" would not even enter into the analysis. There the verbal shift appears to reflect a deeper philosophical distinction.

Consider the following:

(i)   "*S* believes in a strong world government."
(ii) "*S* believes in a united Germany."

Here, S does not believe (i) that there is a strong world government, or (ii) that there is a united Germany. If we attempt to analyze these cases in terms of "belief that," we should favor paraphrases like the following:

- A. S believes that the establishment of a strong world government is possible.
- B. S believes that a strong world government would provide excellent governmental services.
- C. S believes that the establishment of such an institution would be a good thing.

Thus analyzed, the use of "belief in p" is quite similar to that of "hope that p" and quite different from that of "belief that p." Hence, one need not be retreating in conceding that, although the belief that there is a life after death is not justified, the hope that there is, is. Those who *believe in* life after death are not thereby committed to the belief that there is, or will be, a life after death. They must, however, be committed to its possibility. It is not even certain, empirically whether those who believe in life after death usually also believe that there is, or will be, a life after death.

Let us consider, now, the case of belief in God. According to the usual view of the philosophical theologian, the correct analysis of "S believes-in God," in terms of "belief-that," yields:

1. S believes that God exists.
2. S believes that God is able to bring about the highest good, true justice, etc.
3. S believes that it is good that God brings about the highest good, true justice, etc.

The important condition to note is condition 1: "belief in God" is made to entail "belief-that God exists."

Such an analysis is not consistent with the epistemological and religious requirements set down in this essay. To be consistent, the analysis of belief-in God, like the analysis of belief-in life after death, would have to be patterned on the analysis of "S believes in a strong world government." "On that account of "belief-in," "belief-that is not entailed. However, in the world government case, it is part of the background information that what is believed-in does *not* exist. Belief-in God behaves differently. The background assumption is rather that, as there is no sufficient evidence for or against the proposition that God exists, one neither believes nor disbelieves that God exists. Neither the existence nor the non-existence of God is part of the relevant background information.

The following analysis of "S believes in God" conforms to the position advocated in this essay:

1. S believes that it is possible that God exists.
2. S believes that if he exists, God is able to bring about the highest good, true justice, etc.
3. S believes that it would be good if God brought about the highest good, true justice, etc.

This (weak) sense of belief-in God—which is consistent with our epistemological and religious requirements—may be illustrated by an analogy.[41] Imagine a patriot suffering under the yoke of enemy occupation troops. Censorship has been imposed; lines of communication have broken down; there is an aura of mistrust as a result of split loyalties; and so on. It is rumored that a very capable leader has taken control of, and is leading, the resistance movement. However, given the confusion of the moment, these reports can neither be adequately confirmed nor disconfirmed. On the basis of fragmentary evidence and a sense of loyalty to his beleaguered countrymen, the patriot joins the movement. Having judged the situation to be utterly desperate without such a figure, he comes to believe-in the resistance leader (in the weak sense). He stakes his life on this possibility—this HOPE.

Clearly, the parallel religious-belief is not traditionally favored. For example, it is not the orthodox Christian view. One may fairly ask, then, what an orthodox believer (the

Christian, say) would lose or give up if he adopted such an outlook. Before answering that question, however, let us consider, first, what sort of theology may be developed in accord with this new view.

6 A Theology of Hope

Within recent Christian theology, there has developed a movement that has been called the "theology of hope." Jürgen Moltmann, a German Theologian at the center of the development, has explicitly attempted, in his *Theology of Hope,* "to show how theology can set out from hope."[1] According to Moltmann, even in the Resurrection of Jesus, the central event of the Christian faith, the ultimate goal is not yet realized. The death of Jesus promises that death shall be overcome. All of the putative "acts of God" in the Old and New Testaments serve essentially as signposts pointing to the future coming of God. The Christian lives by that promise. He, therefore, lives by hope, much as the patriot in the example of the previous chapter. For faith is HOPE.

The Christian life Moltmann favors has been described by St. Paul, in Romans:

> I consider that the sufferings of this present time are not worth comparing with the glory that is to be revealed to us. For the creation waits with eager longing for the revealing of the sons of God; for the creation was subjected to futility, not of its own will but by the will of him who subjected it in hope; because the creation itself will be set free from its bondage to decay and obtain the glorious liberty of the children of God. We know that the whole creation has been groaning in travail together until now; and not only the creation, but we ourselves, who have the first fruits of the Spirit, groan inwardly as we wait for adoption as sons, the redemption of

our bodies. For in this hope we were saved. Now hope that is seen is not hope. For who hopes for what he sees? But if we hope for what we do not see, we wait for it in patience. (8:18-25)

In II Corinthians, St. Paul states once more that we cannot now see that toward which we strive. The believer does not live in knowledge. There is no demonstrable reality in which our hopes are already fulfilled, to which we can point. There are only events that may be interpreted as signs of a coming New Age.

So we are always of good courage; we know that while we are at home in the body we are away from the Lord, for we walk by faith, not by sight. (5:6-7)

What is described as hope, in Romans, is called faith, in II Corinthians.

I do not intend to deal in a strict and detailed way with Moltmann's theological and exegetical thesis. We shall consider, rather, his statement of his aim, and the features of a theology which "set[s] out from hope" alone. Could such a theology be accepted by a Christian without serious loss— possibly even with benefit? Why might one adopt such a theological position?

An Outline of a Theology of Hope

The fundamental question facing the theologian of hope is Gabriel Marcel's: What constitutes reality if the highest or noblest hopes of man—which are affirmations that reality must contain the means or potency of overcoming tragedy— are to be fulfilled or *vindicated*? Marcel answers that the appropriate responses of hope are vindicated only on the postulate that "there is at the heart of being, beyond all data, beyond all inventories and all calculations, a mysterious principle which is in connivance with me, which cannot but will that which I will, if what I will deserves to be willed and is, in fact, willed by the whole of my being."[2]

Just what is meant by "vindication" can be seen more clearly by contrasting vindication with *justification* and *explanation.* Whereas justifying hope is an epistemological and ethical matter, vindicating hope is metaphysical. It concerns the question: What must the world be like that my HOPE response be a correct response, or that my hope that *p* be not vain?

According to the standard of justification outlined earlier, *S* might be justified in hoping that *p*, without his hope being vindicated. For example, given certain ethical theories and the fact that the object of hope is possible, Kant's hope that a person's happiness be commensurate with his virtue would be justified. Yet, if there is no personal existence beyond the grave, Kant's hope would not be vindicated. On the other hand, a hope may be vindicated without being justified or fully justified. For example, if the best evidence available at time *t* tended to show that *p* might be impossible, the hope that *p* would not be justified, or fully justified at time *t*. Yet *p* might actually be the case, and *S* might even hope that *p* against all reasonable evidence. Hence, *S*'s hope, though not fully justified, might well be finally vindicated.

The issue of vindicating or fulfilling HOPE must also be distinguished from that of explaining our responses of HOPE, or of other related phenomena—in particular, the order and nature of the world that our hope addresses. The argument from design, for instance, attempts to explain the nature of the world by positing God's existence. God, it claims, alone can account for the order that is found in the universe. But the vindication of certain responses regarding the apparent order of the world is quite independent of their explanation. Even if one felt that all the world's phenomena could be adequately explained without appeal to a transcendent order, one might still hold, consistently, that reference to a transcendent reality is required in order to vindicate certain experiences or commitments.

Construing religious-belief as HOPE, in accord with the preceding chapter, the theologian's task is to provide religious adherents with a framework or model for visualizing and expressing their common outlook and aspirations. The theologian determines what reality must be like if the religious-beliefs of the community of the faithful are to be vindicated. The features of the world and of God required for vindication must all find their way into the theologian's picture. Thinking in terms of this picture, or model, is *as-if* thinking.[3] One cannot guarantee a correspondence between the model and what it is supposed to model. However, the theologian pins his hopes upon this correspondence.[4]

How well the model mirrors reality cannot, of course, be tested by any straightforward empirical examination. In developing the theological model, however, all actual events and all conceivable possibilities are accomodated; hence, one cannot disprove the hoped-for correspondence, as in scientific testing, by reference to disconfirming empirical evidence.

The theologian's task is to re-interpret Christian doctrine so that what is considered essential or most important to the faith may be retained. The re-interpretation constitutes an effort to bridge the gap between the original biblical message and the altered patterns of thinking of our own age. Hence, the theologian's task must be pursued anew in each era. The theology of hope is the attempt to be faithful to the essentials of the biblical message while accepting, at least as an initial assumption, the contemporary framework in which the model of science is thought to set constraints on reasonable belief and knowledge. The theologian tries to present a model of reality that can withstand the most stringent criticism and to spell out as well the implications of adhering to that model. He familiarizes himself with the model's implications so that he may inform those who intend to adhere to it what bearing it has for one's view of God, of man, of worship, etc.

Contrary to the usual practice of traditional theologies, the theology of hope begins with eschatology. If we begin with Kant's hope that justice will *ultimately* win out, that is, that individual happiness will be commensurate with virtue, we must ask ourselves at once what kind of world would vindicate that hope. On the argument already supplied, it requires the existence of God and personal survival.

What kind of world is required in order to vindicate the hope that what now appears to be pointless suffering will ultimately prove not to be such, or to vindicate the hope of

Marcel, or of Kierkegaard, or of James, or of the longing of Camus for the special responsiveness of the world. Such hopes appear to be vindicated only by the existence of God. Functionally, the question of God's existence is the question of the possibility of an open future. To deny that there is a God is to deny the framework within which alone men hope that the suffering, tragedy, and injustice that penultimately obtains is ultimately defeated.

Lev Shestov, who is acutally a forerunner of the theology of hope, has said:

> The power of the biblical revelation . . . carries us beyond the limits of all human comprehension and of the possibilities which that comprehension admits. For God, however, the impossible does not exist. God—to speak the language of Kierkegaard, which is that of the Bible—God: this means that there is nothing that is impossible. And despite the Spinozist interdictions, fallen man aspires, in the final analysis, only to the promised "nothing will be impossible for you," only for this does he implore the Creator.[5]

On the model offered by the theologian of hope, God is seen as an omnipotent being, as a being for whom nothing is impossible, whose power is without limit. Ultimate reality transcends whatever can be measured, tested, controlled, understood in accord with the most powerful extension of the methods of science. All human attempts to circumscribe, or limit, the possible are judged therefore in the light of postulating a God for whom all things are possible.

Faith is the courage or audacity to act on the postulate that all things are possible. It is the daring refusal to accept the ultimacy of supposed necessary laws, the refusal to regard the apparently impossible as necessarily impossible. The great contemporary scholar, Mircea Eliade, says quite simply that faith in the Judeo-Christian sense, faith modelled on the faith of Abraham, signifies that "for God all is possible." To possess such a faith signifies, therefore, refusing to circumscribe the boundaries of what is possible for man.

> Since the "invention" of faith, in the Judaeo-Christian sense of the word (= for God all is possible), the man who has left the horizon of

archetypes and repetition can no longer defend himself against that terror except through the idea of God. In fact, it is only by presupposing the existence of God that he conquers, on the one hand, freedom (which grants him autonomy in a universe governed by laws or, in other words, the "inauguration" of a mode of being that is new and unique in the universe) and, on the other hand, the certainty that historical tragedies have a transhistorical meaning, even if that meaning is not always visible for humanity in its present condition. Any other situation of modern man leads, in the end, to despair.[6]

If this is the meaning of faith, then religious faith and hope coalesce. As we saw in our earlier discussion of the phenomenology of hope, one who hopes is committed to the view that the possible must not be prematurely circumscribed. As Kierkegaard maintains, hope is "the passion for the possible." Like faith, hope is the attitude of the adventurer and discoverer, not that of the technician. Like faith, hope challenges what appears obvious and unimpeachable. Like faith, hope affirms a way out, in spite of all obstacles. Christian hope, like faith, is the freedom to decipher the signs of the Resurrection under the apparently contradictory evidence of death.

The putative events of the life of Jesus paradigmatically convey this faith and hope. Son of a poor carpenter, Jesus proclaimed himself the anticipated messiah and attracted a small band of followers—among whom one betrayed him. At the age of thirty-three, he was crucified as a criminal by the authorities. Yet this tragic career has been taken to be the prototype of human experience. For the dying Jesus, there was no guarantee of Easter. So, too, every Christian lives in the hope of the Resurrection despite the apparent betrayal of life, the apparently cruel and ever untimely death.

On the view of a theology of hope, revelation is not a theophany—God's showing himself to someone at a particular time. Revelation is rather an event or series of events seen as signs, or promises, of what is to come. The biblical story of Moses in the desert (Exodus 3) serves as an example. Moses did not see God; he saw only the burning bush, a sign of God's presence. He is told that the Israelites will be freed from slavery and brought to "a land flowing with milk and honey." He asks, Who has promised this? What is his name? The answer given is, "I will be what I will be" (Exodus 3:14). In the New Testament, the ultimate evelation is that Jesus is the Christ. What is seen is apparently a man. What is proclaimed is the coming of a New Age. Those who accept the event as revelatory of the Christ accept the promise, and live in hope in the interim.

On this view, worship is construed as an exercise strengthening individual and corporate commitment to the hope that, in reality, justice, creativity, and goodness will be victorious. In participating in the ritual, one lives as if the model mirrors reality; the object of one's hope is symbolized by the details of one's life. The highest form of worship entails reflection on the attributes of God interpreted by that model. In this way, the religious gain a sense of the holy, the "numinous." For instance, in reciting the revelatory events bearing on the fulfillment of God's promises regarding the Israelites' occupation of the promised land, worshippers keep alive the hope of fulfillment of as yet unfulfilled promises.

Despairing, despite God's omnipotence and mercy, that justice will not ultimately triumph is, therefore, to be construed as a form of the primary theological sin. Even if one's own life or, for that matter all of human history *appears* to be tragic, one can continue to hope—and one's religious intuitions require that one must—that tragedy be not the final word, that the appearance be not the reality. Conversely, the hope that guides the believer's life (the "faith by which he lives") is simply that no obstacle, including death, will ultimately be insurmountable by the forces of creativity, justice, and compassion. Hell, the ultimate consequence of sin, is a life devoid of all hope. Hell is the loss of all hope. In the *Divine Comedy,* Dante portrays this vividly by placing over the entrance to hell the words "lasciate ogni speranza, voi ch'entrate" ("all hope abandon, ye who enter here") ("Inferno" III).

Here, as in traditional theologies, prayer is "talking to" God; but it is accompanied by the hope rather than the belief that one's prayers are being heard. Analogies suggest themsleves. For example, a woman may write to her husband who is actually either a prisoner of war or dead. She may, rationally, compose letters to him, hoping—without yet be- lieving—that he will read them. Similarly, we may imagine someone on his deathbed, whose condition is such that we cannot actually tell whether he is dead or alive. We could still talk to him, hoping, without believing, that he was alive and could hear what was said. On this view, the religious believer might ask God to intervene in the world, though, perhaps with less confidence than orthodox believers in the results obtained.

On a theology of hope, the ideal religious life is pursued by those who are not content with anything less than the abso- lute good, the *summum bonum*. The believer is guided by this ideal. To be sure, he will have hopes and desires for many other things. But he will control his attachment to finite things. For example, if he responds in a religiously correct manner, a believer will not permit the tragedy of the illness or death of a loved one to lead him to despair of life, or to find life meaningless. In preparation for such contingencies, the religious life requires less than total commitment to anything finite. One's desires, one's hopes, one's disappoint- ments must accord with one's ultimate hope. Any conflicting desire must be suitably modified, for the religious life is essen- tially centered on the hope for the highest good. With charac- teristic exaggeration, Kierkegaard affirms: "Earthly hope must be killed; only then can one be saved by true hope."[7]

A theology of hope is intended as an aid to living such a life. By making the implications for one's life explicit and by filling in the details of the model memorably, the theology helps one to feel at home with its directives. It assists one in managing the religious and moral aspects of his life.

The conception of God and the eschaton provides the theologian of hope with a vantage point from which to evaluate and question the social and moral order and presuppositions of his own time. For example, all conceptions of justice are measured by the ideal of the eschaton. Hence, since all present arrangements and standards are entirely provisional, a critical attitude is in order. Living by the promise of the *summum bonum*, one is disposed to work in the present historical situation into closer approximation to the ideal. One can be satisfied with nothing less. As Jacques Ellul says:

> The challenge of hope is the introduction into a closed age, into a tight security, into an autocephalous organization, into an autonomous economic system, into totalitarian politics, of an opening, a breech, a heteronomy, an uncertainty, and a question. . . . The revolutionary act of hope is, and can only be, the opening up of situations which want to stay closed, and the contradiction of systems.[8]

From the point of view of a theology of hope, the great mistake of the historical Church was to become a support for the status quo, to organize present power, to become prosperous and to settle in, to rest and wait in comfort and security. Instead of remaining a force for change, a critic of false absolutes and of the pretensions of system builders—part of its genuine mission—the Church gave up its venture and its vision, made its own claims to false absolutes and, through its own systematizers, advanced its own pretensions to knowledge. From the perspective of a theology of hope, it has been lulled asleep by a false sense of security.

This brief outline of a theology of hope could easily be expanded. Its actual development, however, is more the task of the theologian than the philosopher; although having touched on some of the basic doctrines favored by any such theology, it has already served our present purpose.

Recent theologies of hope with which I am familiar have not typically confined themselves within the epistemological constraints of this essay—in spite of the fact that the avoidance of epistemological irresponsibility has to some extent motivated their development. Also, theologies of hope are often less ambitious than the name would suggest. For example, merely to attempt to show that the doctrine of eschatology is central to a genuine Christian theology has been taken as the sufficient mark of a theology of hope. Hence, much of the theologian's task still lies before him, once a theology of hope is thought capable of providing, for our time, a viable re-interpretation of the biblical message.

In order to see whether it would, in fact, be an adequate and attractive alternative, we shall, first, consider traditional Christian theology, and then, finally, compare the two.

A Theology of Hope and Traditional Christian Theology

On the assumption that we are clear, now, about the nature of religion and the nature of a theology of hope—about what they do and do not commit us to, about what they offer and do not offer—we may ask whether a theology of hope would be an acceptable Christian theology. Certainly, it is not an orthodox Christian theology. For instance, it cannot consistently offer objective certainty regarding its basic tenets. It offers a venture, not certainty; correspondingly, it construes a religious-belief as a species of hope, not as a species of belief. Hope, then, becomes the initial motivation of the religious life.

In much of the primary literature of Christianity, and in orthodox Christian theology, things are reversed. Christianity appears, there, to offer certainty rather than a venture. Religious-belief becomes a species of strong belief that initiates the distinctively Christian life. Hope is simply entailed by one's belief. One's religious development moves from faith, or belief, to high hope; that is, the hope that p (e.g., p = "I am saved") depends upon one's belief-that, or even certainty that q (e.g., q = "God is loving and omnipotent"). Reference to hope in the primary literature and in orthodox theology is essentially reference to *hope-in* (to trust, or have confidence in) God's omnipotence and mercy rather than to *hope-that* God exists or is merciful, etc. Such hope cannot but presuppose belief regarding God's existence, God's nature, God's plan of salvation, etc.

A brief account of some details of the Old and New Testaments (based on the exegetical work of Jürgen Moltmann[9] and C. F. D. Moule[10]) will permit us to make explicit the conceptual relations that hold in biblical thought between faith, certainty, and hope.

God is reported to have made a covenant with Abraham, that his descendents would become a great nation[11] and receive a land of their own.[12] On the strength of this promise, Abraham and those who share his faith look *expectantly* toward the future. God (Yahweh) is believed to keep his promises, so the faithful feel *secure.*[13] Complacency however, is not acceptable; the covenant makes moral demands on men as well.[14] Nor does their conviction free them from the ordinary vicissitudes of life.[15]

Faith in God's promises and faithfulness lead the prophets of the exile to hope for the age of the Messiah when the "kingdom of God" is to be established.[16] Their hope is for an unending age of justice and peace under the rule of Yahweh. Daniel speaks of the coming of such an age, after great struggle and upheaval. The favorable signs include the coming of the Messiah and the resurrection of the dead.

The New Testament writers were convinced that the new age had actually dawned. The man Jesus was proclaimed the long hoped-for Messiah.[17] It was believed that, in his coming all the promises previously revealed were, or would be, fulfilled. For example, the man Jesus arose from the grave—a direct fulfillment of one of the Messianic prophesies. Hence, it was expected that he would return to initiate the end of time.[18] There would, then, be a resurrection of the dead.[19] Thus, in the Revelation to John, the details of the reign of God provide the vivid content of what the believer *confidently supposes he knows.*

The symbol of the anchor[20] has caught the imagination of Christians through the ages. It expresses succinctly the function of hope in biblical and classical Christian thought. In the battering storms of life, the wayfarer's *hope in* God remains an anchor in a stormy sea—a constant source of security, calm and respite. One's hope for the future—a future not of this world alone[21] —is fastened to God's promise and faithfulness, most clearly demonstrated in the life of Jesus as the resurrected Christ.[22]

In short, in the biblical literature, one hopes for the new age, the coming of the reign of Yahweh. But one also awaits this development with *confidence and expectation*—even *certainty*. The believer's hope rests in what he takes to be God's undeniable benevolence and omnipotence. The believer is sure that God will not fail. So, although he lives in hope, in a sense he claims more than hope. He has a sense of security and assurance about the future.[23] In the biblical view, faith is logically prior to hope. One's hope is formed *on the basis* of his faith and his belief that God exists and that God is at least benevolent and omnipotent.

The usual accounts of hope in the biblical literature are not really paradigmatic, like those described in the chapter that deals with the phenomenology of hope. Some accounts, like St. Paul's of Abraham's "hope against hope"[24] and of hope in the unseen as a sign of our endurance,[25] do fit quite naturally with our description of hope. However, the courage, the daring, the commitment of Abraham—depending (on Paul's account) on the absence of a solid basis for hope, is hardly matched in most biblical discussions. For, although the believer speaks of his hope, he usually claims to have more than hope. He lives in *certainty* that nothing "can separate us from the love of God."[26] He *knows* that his "labor is not in vain."[27]

Let us turn now from this over-view to take a brief look at some representative theological accounts regarding faith, belief, hope and certainty.

St. Thomas Aquinas, who, as we saw, took as a necessary condition for hope the condition that the object of one's hope must be difficult but possible to attain, maintained that Christians primarily hope for their own salvation. One's salvation is a good attained only through arduous labor. But because of personal limitations, the difficulty of the effort, and the extreme futurity of the goal, one normally cannot be sure of salvation—even though, on the strength of faith, one *can* be sure of God's mercy and omnipotence, and that the kingdom of God will prevail in spite of all. The possible inadequacy of one's personal effort must leave one uncertain and insecure.[28] Insecurity itself may be overcome by the firm resolution to persevere,[29] by one's commitment to strive for eternal life. In that way, one's life is organized and directed toward one goal. And that unity of purpose, coupled with trust in God's mercy and power, provides a sense of calm and satisfaction—always regarding an unknown personal future.

One's hope lies in "divine omnipotence and mercy."[30] That God is omnipotent and merciful is known through faith and with certainty. It is on this certainty that one bases the hope of salvation. Hence, faith is logically prior to hope.[31] Aquinas appears to argue thus because the object of hope must be taken to be possible—"the mere fact of hoping would be out of the question if the hoped-for good did not appear possible."[32] But the Christian's object would not seem possible to him if he did not know by faith that there exists a merciful and omnipotent God. "It is thus apparent that faith comes before hope."[33]

A comment is in order here. We have seen in the analysis of hoping that God exists, seen that hoping for eternal salvation, or for a life in which happiness is commensurate with virtue, does not actually require believing that God exists; it requires only the hope that God exists or the belief that possibly, God exists. But neither that hope nor that belief need be propositions of faith. Hence, contrary to Aquinas, faith is not a logical prerequisite of the hope for salvation.

Of course, if one feels secure in the general mercy and omnipotence of God, it takes less daring to muster one's hope for a share of God's mercy than it does on the strength of believing only in the possibility of a merciful and omnipotent God. Lacking the certainty of faith, one cannot help but find despair a very great temptation. Clearly, therefore, the certainty of faith aids those who are weak on hope and slow to venture.

In the Aristotelian manner, Aquinas views the virtue of hope as a mean between the extremes of despair and presumption. Both extremes are sins against hope.[34] To despair, no matter how evil one may be, is to belittle God's goodness and power.[35] But to expect to be saved by God despite one's sins is to act presumptuously, to belittle God's justice—which entails punishing the sinner.[36]

According to Catholic orthodoxy, based on the Thomist theology, it seems that we have knowledge of God's attributes and of what is required for a grasp of God's plan of salvation. But we cannot have knowledge of our own salvation; we can only hope for that. On the orthodox Catholic view, expressed for instance by the Council of Trent, the Reformist position adopted by Martin Luther and John Calvin erred on the side of presumption. For in accord with Reformation theology, one may sometimes rely on more than hope. Through grace, a believer can actually know with certainty that he has been saved. There is, therefore, a considerable psychological difference in the attitudes of Catholic and Reformed theologians regarding the certainty of one's own salvation. Luther allegedly discovered that God's grace would certainly override his justice in determining the eternal fate of the faithful. This was, in fact, the *good* news of the Gospel. According to Luther, the revealed message assures us that we sinners are acceptable to God, even though, by the strict standards of divine justice, we are clearly unacceptable.

Calvin answers the orthodox charge that his claim that the faithful possess an indisputable knowledge of personal salvation is a "rash presumption."[37] He claims that when each true Christian receives the Holy Spirit he receives assurance of his salvation as well.[38] Speaking of the scholastic position, he says:

A fine confidence of salvation is left to us, if by moral conjecture we judge that at the present moment we are in grace, but we know not what will become of us tomorrow! The apostle speaks far otherwise: "I am surely convinced that neither angels, nor powers, nor principalities, nor death, nor life, nor things present, nor things to come . . . will separate us from the love by which the Lord embraces us in Christ." (Rom. 8:38-39) They try to escape with a trifling solution, praying that the apostle had his assurance from a special revelation. But they are held too tightly to escape. For there he is discussing those benefits which come to all believers in common from faith, not those things which he exclusively experiences.[39]

Nevertheless, despite the Christ-event, the efficacy of the Holy Spirit, and the true believer's certain knowledge of salvation, Calvin insists that the Christian must live in hope.[40] By hope, Calvin means, however, no more than *expectation* —"hope is nothing else than the expectation of those things which faith has believed to have been truly promised by God."[41] He does not accept the view that the hope that p is incompatible with certainty that p. According to Calvin's theology, therefore, the Christian does not live in hope (in our sense); he already has knowledge superior to hope.

Recent Neo-orthodox Protestant theology understands "hope" very much in Calvin's sense. For example, Emil Brunner says:

> In our everyday experience to "hope for" means the expectation of a wished-for event in the future. There is therefore always implied in it the element of complete uncertainty. But the Christian hope is of another kind. It is no uncertain expectation based on a wish, but the expectation of the future that has its basis in the known will of God and therefore shares in the certainty of his knowledge.[42]

Contemporary theologians of hope find it rather strange that so many Christian theorists have all but bypassed hope in developing their systematic theologies. Clearly, the reason for this, sketched in our short overview, is that the Christian makes knowledge-claims regarding the future and his relationship to the future which are cognitively superior to whatever hope could justify. Hope is transcended, for the Resurrected Christ provides the Christian with a guarantee of the future. He lives in joyous expectation rather than in mere hope. He looks ahead not merely with resolve, but with an unshakable confidence as well.

A theology of hope offers no grounds for such confidence or such joyous expectation. If these are psychologically essential to the Christian stance (certainly, they are to the theologies we have just sampled), then a theology of hope cannot be a Christian theology. If the primary function of Christianity is to provide cosmic security and acceptance, then a theology of hope will inevitably fail to serve that purpose. But if, on the other hand, a Christian theology functions to provide a sense of the direction of life, of its meaning and purpose (not a privileged solace or special knowledge of any sort), then (I believe) a theology of hope will prove adequate for Christian needs.

Deciding Between a Theology of Hope and a Theology of Belief

As we have already noted, Søren Kierkegaard distinguishes between those religions that are based on Socratic ignorance (Religiousness A) and those that are based on what he calls the category of the absurd (Religiousness B). According to Kierkegaard, Religiousness B is the specifically Christian faith. The difference between the two may, without much distortion, be marked as the difference between a religion based on hope—conforming with the epistemological requirements set forth in this essay—(Religiousness A) and a religion based on belief or certainty (Religiousness B). Hence, we may use Kierkegaard's distinction in order to focus finally on just what the underlying issues are affecting the choice of a theology of hope or a theology of belief.

In the previous section, we saw that a very strong theme in the primary literature and in classical theological views is one of certainty. On those views, the Christian is quite certain that God exists, that God reigns, and that particular actions of God affecting human history guarantee the eternal happiness of believers. "Actuality, i.e., the fact that this or that actually occurred, is the subject of faith. . ."[43] Religiousness B, or traditional Christian faith, and theologies of belief are based on supposed actualities rather than mere possibilities. A distinctively Christian assertion implies factual claims regarding a particular set of historical events. The Christian reasons that, because Christ rose, men shall rise at the appointed time. One moves beyond hope to assurance regarding a life after death—on the strength of the supposed significance of the historical resurrection of Christ.

Since he was not willing to adopt a religion and theology of hope (Religiousness A), Kierkegaard construes Religiousness A as a condition of Religiousness B.[44] One must first realize, Kierkegaard insists, that nothing short of striving for the highest good, for eternal happiness, will permit one to rest content. Then, and only then he says, will the believer be open to the dialectical and the paradoxical claims of a distinctly Christian religiousness (B).

> When the eternal happiness as the absolute *telos* has become for him absolutely the only comfort, and when accordingly his relationship to it is reduced to its minimum through the attainment of existential depth . . . and yet this minimum and this possibility are absolutely more than everything else to him, then is the appropriate time to begin with the dialectical.[45]

In A, although it is not known whether the highest good or eternal happiness is attainable, the believer grasps the possibility and is prepared to risk all for it. He does so because he can be satisfied with nothing less. Less would leave his life desparate and meaninglessness. Religiously, to esteem anything less would be sheer idolatry.

In B, the Christ-event—the life, death, and resurrection of Jesus the Christ—guarantees the believer's eternal happiness. How does it do so? How can a mere historical event provide one with grounds for such certainty? In the primary literature and the representative theologies, as we have seen, it is the Christ-event itself that insures that certainty. But on the criterion of justified belief favored in this essay, and on the implicit criterion adopted by Kierkegaard, no one is rationally justified in making an historical event (whose truth-value must be determined by the use of objective investigative techniques) the basis for a belief about what is one's *ultimate* concern. The evidence for an historical event cannot be as strong, in principle, as the degree of assent required regarding whatever would form the basis of one's ultimate concern. Kierkegaard says:

> The contradiction first emerges in the fact that the subject in the extremity of such subjective passion (in the concern for an eternal happiness) has to base this upon an historical knowledge which at its maximum remains an approximation. . . . To require the greatest possible subjective passion, to the point of hating father and mother, and then to put this together with an historical knowledge, which at its maximum can only be an approximation—that is the contradiction.[46]

From the point of view of rational justification of belief the position to be defended appears to be worse off than ever. Appeal to the putative historical fact that Jesus Christ rose from the grave about 33 A.D. and ascended into heaven runs contrary to the requirement to apportion the degree of one's assent to a proposition to the supporting evidence. Kierkegaard regards the disproportion between the two as an advantage. His "solution" is simply to admit that being a Christian (Religiousness B) cannot be shown to be rational. Contrary to the thesis of this essay, Kierkegaard feels that we would be well advised to abandon compatibilist interpretations.

> Christianity has declared itself to be the eternal essential truth which has come into being in time. It has proclaimed itself as the *Paradox,* and it has required of the individual the inwardness of faith in relation to that which stamps itself as an offense to the Jews and a folly to the Greek—and an absurdity to the understanding.[47]

If one is to be a Christian, he must believe against the understanding—"which is like rolling a burden up a mountain."[48] The Christian uses his reason to determine what is at stake in risking his faith, and what rational basis there may be for it. Finding no basis for rational belief, he must, against the understanding, firmly believe nonetheless.

Not only are the grounds for belief insufficient; *what* is

believed—the Paradox: that God existed in the man Jesus—cannot even be understood. The Paradox to be believed reason cannot understand, beyond understanding that it cannot understand *that*. The Paradox is not a logically contradictory notion; nor is it nonsense. The believer cannot believe nonsense. "Nonsense . . . he cannot believe against the understanding, for precisely the understanding will discern that it is nonsense and will prevent him from believing it; but he makes so much use of the understanding that he becomes aware of the incomprehensible, and then he holds to this, believing against the understanding."[49]

We may, interpreting the primary biblical literature in the traditional Christian manner, and adopting our own criterion for justified belief, fairly conclude that Kierkegaard's epistemological evaluation of distinctly Christian belief is quite correct. It *cannot* be rationally justified. Kierkegaard turned this conclusion to advantage. He simply viewed inwardness and the paradoxical as essential elements of the religious. Hence, since paradoxically, it demanded *both* certainty *and* the radical insecurity which promotes inwardness, Kierkegaard concluded that Christianity (Religiousness B) was superior to Religiousness A.

To my mind, Kierkegaard has very honestly and effectively demonstrated that a distinctly Christian theology of belief obliges one to reject every effort to reconcile religious-belief with ordinary criteria of reasonably justified belief. Kierkegaard's willingness to believe against the understanding may be the most straightforward response for a Christian to adopt. Nevertheless, this bold but utterly irresponsible epistemological position has never had more than very limited appeal to those who support the ideal of rationality.

For those who are religious, and who—for whatever reasons—are neither disposed toward Christian orthodoxy nor willing to abandon the sort of epistemological principles here favored, the position developed in this essay provides a possible alternative. It is a religious alternative that allows at once both for rationality and for a passionate response. It calls for discipleship short of crucifying one's reason. In place of that, one merely foregoes a sense of cosmic security and the certainty of orthodox Christian claims.

A theology of hope is particularly attractive in our own time. For instance, it embraces common phenomenon of intellectual doubt as an integral and healthy feature of religious life. Uncertainty regarding basic tenets need not be repressed, need not produce guilt feelings—more likely, in fact, in the context of a consistent theology of belief. Furthermore, it is hospitable to another widespread phenomenon, what may be called the experience of the *absence* of God—joined at the same time with a longing for God. A theology of belief that stresses religious experience, or encounters between the human and the divine is not a live option for those who share the sense of the absence of God. But a theology of hope would be a live option. It actually embraces this contemporary experience. As Jacques Ellul says, in *Hope in Time of Abandonment:*

> When God is turned away, then, in the desert of information, nothing more is possible but hope. That is the only path open to us today. Philosophical or theological dissertations no longer have any possible meaning or substance for us. Surely hope is a theological virtue. It is the virtue for a time which has no faith, no word, and no escape.[50]

In addition to expressing a common experience, a theology of hope inherently restricts theological excess by its epistemological skepticism. For example, a theology of hope cannot condone dogmatism; one realizes emphatically that the truth of one's ultimate commitments is neither guaranteed nor well-established. Clearly, one of the most telling reasons why so many thoughtful people have disagreed with Kant and Mill, and have repudiated religion has been the persistence of religious dogmatism and its undeniably evil results (e.g., as in the Crusades and the Inquisition—events made possible by the conviction of a privileged relationship to God and God's truth).

Another scale of comparison between the two theologies

concerns moral accountability. Since hopes are appropriately judged by moral criteria, a theology of hope can obviously be held morally accountable. As we have seen, however, whereas hopes may be correctly evaluated morally, beliefs about putative facts and states of affairs cannot. For example, if the doctrine of the eternal torment of sinners and unbelievers is construed as a possible object of hope, it may be judged unacceptable on current moral theories. If, on the other hand, it is taken to reflect a matter of revealed fact, one might condemn it as contrary to moral interests; but one could not say correctly that the mere *belief* that eternal torment awaits the sinner is itself morally reprehensible. One would have to challenge the belief on the evidence. But, in adopting a theology of belief, one may easily relax the criterion of justified belief to a more permissive level than the Lockean, common-sense, criterion. One may even opt for an esoteric notion of religious evidence. In short, epistemological controls are, ironically, much more difficult to insert in a theology of belief than in a theology of hope. But without them, the orderly and legitimate criticism of religious-belief and theology becomes impossible to specify. Most would agree (I believe) that theologies ought to be answerable. That a theology of hope can meet such constraints is a point in its favor.

If one does not favor a theology of hope—concerned withal with of the rationality of his religious outlook—he probably favors liberalizing the criterion of justified belief. As we saw very early on, that criterion should perhaps be liberalized somewhat. If, however, it is adjusted sufficiently to justify traditional Christian theologies of belief, we should not be able to exclude all sorts of strange beliefs unacceptable even to those we have accommodated. Hence, whereas a traditional Christian theology of belief cannot satisfy the requirements of any reasonably more permissive criterion of justified belief, a theology of hope may satisfy both the strictest, and any reasonably more permissive, criterion of justified belief.

Collectively, then, these are good reasons why those who

harbor transcendent hopes should opt for a theology of hope as the model of their aspirations.

According to ancient Greek mythology, Zeus gave to mankind a cask filled with all good things. However, beguiled by curiosity, they opened the cask. Before all the good things could escape, the cask was quickly closed. Only hope remained. I have tried to show that hope—the one remaining gift of the gods—affords a sufficient cognitive foundation for an attractive religious position capable of providing contemporary man with the ultimate guidance for his life.

Notes

Introduction

1. Immanuel Kant, *Critique of Pure Reason*, trans. by Norman Kemp Smith (New York: St. Martin's Press, 1965), A805 = B833.
2. John Stuart Mill, *Theism*, ed. by Richard Taylor (Indianapolis: The Bobbs-Merrill Co., Inc., 1957), p. 78.
3. *Ibid*. Mill does not develop a criterion for justified and/or justifiable hopes that *p* (where *p* is some proposition or event). He simply offers a brief utilitarian justification of hopefulness or optimism.
4. Jürgen Moltmann is the foremost representative of the group that bases its claims concerning hope on the exegetical work of biblical scholars. See Jürgen Moltmann, *Theology of Hope: On the Ground and the Implications of a Christian Eschatology* (New York: Harper & Row, 1967).
5. The theologians in this group have not worked out any clear position and have no obvious spokesman. One can get a feeling for this view in some of the articles in Martin E. Marty and Dean G. Peerman, eds., *New Theology*, No. 5 (New York: The Macmillan Company, 1968).
6. William Hamilton, "Thursday's Child," in *Radical Theology and the Death of God*, ed. by Thomas J. J. Altizer and William Hamilton (Indianapolis: The Bobbs-Merrill Co., Inc., 1966), p. 87.

Chapter 1

1. A philosophical or logical analysis of the concept of hope can be seen as trying to determine what must be the case for us to say correctly that someone hopes. Speaking roughly, providing an analysis is working out an equation. On the one side is the concept hope and on the other side is the set of conditions (called the necessary and jointly sufficient conditions) which represent the analysis of the concept. If the right hand side can be said to balance the left hand side the analysis

is a success. The test for balance is as follows: If whenever you want to affirm what is on the right you also want to affirm what is on the left and whenever you wish to deny the one you wish to deny the other and whenever you are unsure of the one you are unsure of the other, balance has been achieved.

2. David Hume, *A Treatise of Human Nature*, L. A. Selby-Bigge edition (Oxford: At the Clarendon Press, 1888), Bk. II, Pt. III, sect. IX, pp. 438-48.

3. Hume, as well as other classical writers such as Hobbes and Aquinas, speak of "passions." But something quite different from our present-day notion of passions is meant. That this is the case is clearly seen by the fact that Hume speaks of the "calm passions." However, with our present use of the word "passion" such an expression appears to be contradictory. Quite clearly the connotations of the word "passions" have changed considerably since the eighteenth century. Given our present-day understanding of the term, "passion," which includes the aspect of intense feeling and agitation, to apply it to hope, despair, or fear *in all cases* would be inaccurate. The term "emotion" can be applied quite naturally.

4. *Ibid.*, p. 440.

5. Hume speaks of opposing or contrary emotions. Joy and grief are opposite emotions as are hope and fear. Hume is, no doubt, following Aristotle and others who earlier wrote of the opposition of emotions. (Cf. Aristotle, *Rhetorica*, Bk. II, especially 1377b21-1378a5, 138a12-1383b11). In Aristotle's discussion of opposite emotions, "opposite" has the same sense as it has in the Square of Opposition. (Cf. Aristotle, *Metaphysics,* Bk. X, 4, 5. 1055a2-1056b2). The opposite emotions of hope and fear are not contradictories because they are not exhaustive alternatives. Quite clearly a person need not either hope or fear that the Mets will win the World Series in baseball next season. However, hope and fear are thought to be contraries (opposites). That is, they are taken to be exclusive alternatives. It is thought (although, perhaps, incorrectly) that a person cannot *simultaneously* hope and fear that a particular event will occur.

6. Hume, p. 443.

7. Although we must be very careful to distinguish "hoping that . . ." and "hoping in . . ." because the grammatical difference is based on a logical difference, it is immaterial whether we use the locution "hoping that . . ." or "hoping for . . ." It is immaterial because the locutions can be interchanged without any change in meaning. Consider: "We hope that the weather will be good for the picnic tomorrow." "We hope for good weather for the picnic tomorrow." Or: "I hope that our side wins" etc.

8. William Alston, in "Feelings," *Philosophical Review*, January, 1969, pp. 3-34, has demonstrated, I believe, that one is misguided in trying to reduce wants and desires into logically simpler components of

feelings and dispositions—for feelings and dispositions toward behavior are not logically simpler. Hence it seems that it is best to settle for desires or wants as the primitives in a logical analysis of "hope." That is not to say, of course, that to show the ways in which to have a given desire is to be disposed to have certain feelings or behave in certain ways under certain circumstances would not contribute to our understanding. What is being denied is that we are making that contribution by exhibiting simpler components of the concept.

9. J. P. Day, "Hope," *American Philosophical Quarterly,* vol. 6, no. 2 (April, 1969), pp. 89-102. On p. 89 he says: "I disagree with Hume that Hope is an emotion. . . . Hope involves (1) desiring and (2) estimating a probability. . . . The estimation of probabilities is plainly not an emotion." Day gives no argument for the claim that the *estimation* of probabilities is a necessary element of hope. But he uses it as a major premise in his argument that, contrary to the views of philosophers like Aristotle, Aquinas, Descartes, and Hume, hope is not an emotion.

10. For an account of precisely what is meant in this context by "contrary," see footnote number 5, chapter 1 above.

11. Thomas Hobbes, "Of the Passions," *Leviathan* (Indianapolis: The Bobbs-Merril Company, Inc., 1958), Pt. I, chapter 6.

12. René Descartes, *The Passions of the Soul,* Part II, art. LVIII, in *The Philosophical Works of Descartes,* trans. by Elizabeth S. Haldane and G. R. T. Ross (Cambridge: At the Unviersity Press, 1968), vol. II, p. 359.

13. J. M. O. Wheatley, "Wishing and Hoping," *Analysis,* vol. XVIII (June, 1958), pp. 121-31.

14. St. Thomas Aquinas, *Summa Theologiae,* 1a2ae. 40-44, trans. and ed. by John Patrick Reid, O. P. (London: Blackfriars, 1965), vol. 21. Aquinas discusses hope as one of the emotions in 1a2ae and as one of the theological virtues in 2a2ae.

15. *Ibid.,* 1a2ae. 40, 1; vol. 21, p.5.

16. Many of our hopes, perhaps most, are directed toward the future. Hence, someone might wish to argue that hopes concerning the past or present are simply special cases and that the important thing to note is that there is a future element in these cases as well. It might be maintained that in the above case the person who hopes is really hoping that evidence *will* be forthcoming to verify his hopes.

But is it necessarily the case that when, say, I hope that a friend is well again now or hope that I was not an embarrassment to the host at the party I am really hoping that evidence will be forthcoming which will show that my friend is well or that I am not an embarrassment to the host at the party? Quite likely, in both of these cases, I *also* hope that such evidence will be forthcoming. The hope about forthcoming evidence is a hope I might have besides the hope that my friend is well again or that I was not an embarrassment to my host.

That these are *distinct* hopes can be seen by looking at examples so constructed that the person hoping is quite certain that no future evidence is forthcoming. Consider the following: Mr. Jones and Mr. Smith have been life-long friends but, in a fit of anger, Jones falsely and irrationally accuses Smith of callousness and deceit in their relationship. Hard feelings result. Jones, knowing that he is to blame for the unpleasant situation, sends Smith a note of apology and a request that their friendship be renewed. But very shortly after receiving the note from Jones—before he (Smith) has a chance to speak with anyone—Smith dies. Now Jones *hopes*, even though Jones (correctly) believes that evidence will not be forthcoming, that Smith had accepted Jones' note in the spirit in which it was written. Here is a case in which one hopes even though there is no future consideration. Certainly, many such cases could be constructed. It follows that it is not necessary that the object of hope be in some way in the future.

17. *Ibid*.

Chapter 2

1. Marcel's most complete discussion of this topic is his essay, "Sketch of a Phenomenology and a Metaphysics of Hope," in *Homo Viator*, trans. by Emma Craufurd (New York: Harper & Row, Publishers, 1962). The present discussion is based primarily on this essay but, as will be evident, reference is made to a number of Marcel's other articles and books as well.

Marcel's discussion of the phenomenology of hope—although suggestive—is rather opaque. He gives few hints as to his methodology or the structure of his argument. He often casually conjoins phenomenological and psychological analyses with comments about the epistemic and moral right to hope for something and with putative metaphysical and religious implications regarding hope. One also finds contradictions and terminological shifts. Hence, if an interpreter wishes to provide a consistent and clear account of Marcel's position, he must go beyond Marcel's actual statements.

Any such interpretation could hardly be supposed to be the correct interpretation; alternative interpretations doubtless could be supported. Hence, I do not here claim to be providing the most accurate account of Marcel's view. This is an attempt, rather, to present a plausible and consistent reading without straying too far from what appears to be Marcel's intended meaning. In short, our concern is more with making sense of the topic at hand than of determining precisely what Marcel actually meant in his more obscure passages. His discussion, then is to be used chiefly as a springboard.

2. Hoping for something or hoping that something is the case should not be confused with hopefulness in general or a disposition to be hopeful. Of some people we say: "He always looks on the bright side

of things." For example, there is the hackneyed "definition" of the optimist as the person who describes a glass as half full of liquid rather than half empty. The inveterate pessimist, given the same glass of liquid, would describe it as half empty. There are people who simply have a general psychological propensity to look on the favorable side of things. However, regardless of whether a person has or does not have a general propensity or disposition to look on the bright side, a person can have particular hopes.

3. Gabriel Marcel, *Homo Viator*, p. 29.

4. Those who study suicide often emphasize that the loss of hope is the most significant factor to be investigated. For example, Maurice L. Farber says in the chapter entitled "A Disease of Hope" in his *Theory of Suicide* (New York: Funk & Wagnalls, 1968): "The evidence that it is hope (with its components) that is the variable most powerfully and proximally related to suicide is exceedingly strong. The clinical evidence appears in the work of many students of suicide, although the concept may not be labeled as hope nor its full theoretical implications developed. In our intensive interviews with those who had attempted suicide the centrality of hope and its destruction in case after case was impressive" (p. 17). Stating that "many suicide notes reveal the loss of hope and the unacceptability of the future outlook," Farber cites the example of Harriet Westbrook Shelley who wrote, after being abandoned by her poet husband: "Too wretched to exert myself, lowered in the opinion of everyone, why should I drag out a miserable existence? embittered by past recollections and no one ray of hope to rest on for the future." (p. 18). Another recent study—*The End of Hope*, by Arthur L. Kobler and Ezra Stotland (New York: The Free Press of Glencoe, 1974)—also sees suicide in terms of "the loss of purpose and hope," and considers how those interacting with suicidal persons can find "new bases for hope."

5. *Homo Viator*, p. 32.

6. *Ibid.*, p. 58.

7. Gabriel Marcel, *Mystery of Being*, vol. II: *Faith and Reality*, trans. by René Hague (Chicago: Henry Regnery Co., 1960), pp. 178-79.

8. In the next chapter this special experience of hope is to be referred to explicitly in a discussion of the religious person's response to evidence against theism (such as cases of suffering). In a theology of hope, the response just outlined to (perceived) suffering and tragedy forms the experiential basis for seeking a relationship with God.

9. In speaking here of logical possibilities, I purposely avoid the issue of whether or not persons can "freely" choose either (i) or (ii). Very likely even if persons can make choices of this kind, they need not make a conscious decision. It is more likely to be spontaneous and non-deliberative.

10. *Homo Viator*, p. 37.

11. *Homo Viator*, p. 60; *Mystery of Being*, vol. II, p. 181.

12. *Homo Viator*, p. 36.

13. *Ibid.*, p. 40.

14. *Ibid.*, p. 33.

15. *Ibid.*, p. 34.

16. Cf. Margaret Boden, "Optimism," *⸱sophy*, vol. 41 (1966). Miss Boden considers Leibniz to be a good example of "a genuine form of optimism" (p. 296). The account of optimism which she presents supports the thesis argued here that the basis for optimism is a supposed objective view as to what is desirable or good and what the facts are which support the optimist's claim (pp. 292-92).

17. Cf. *Mystery of Being*, vol. II, p. 262. In Marcel's terminology, HOPE deals with a mystery and optimism with a problem. Marcel says: "When I am dealing with a problem I am trying to discover a solution that can become common property, that consequently can, at least in theory, be rediscovered by anybody at all." A mystery does not have the public, objective characteristic.

18. This example illustrates in a down-to-earth way Marcel's claim that hope is not so much a wish or an obstinate desire as it is a "prophetic affirmation." Cf. *Being and Having*, p. 79; *Homo Viator*, p. 53.

19. *Being and Having*, p. 79; cf. also *Homo Viator*, p. 51; and Gabriel Marcel, "On the Ontological Mystery," *The Philosophy of Existence* (London: The Harvill Press, 1948), p. 20, for further discussion by Marcel of calculation and HOPE.

20. *Mystery of Being*, vol. II, p. 181.

21. *Homo Viator*, p. 55.

22. Søren Kierkegaard, *Fear and Trembling* and *The Sickness Unto Death*, trans. by Walter Lowrie, (Garden City, New York: Doubleday & Company, Inc., 1954), pp. 150-51.

23. Paul Tillich, *Systematic Theology* (3 vols.; Chicago: University of Chicago Press, 1957), vol. II, p. 75.

Chapter 3

1. There is a use of "believe" in which it is used as a retreat from certainty: "Well, I'm not certain that *p*, but I do believe that *p*. I should be surprised if not-*p*"; or, "I guess that I don't *know* that *p* but I believe that *p*." This use may show that certainty is not a necessary condition for belief. But clearly it does not show that certainty is logically incompatible with belief.

2. Cf. A. Phillips Griffiths, "On Belief," in *Knowledge and Belief*, ed. by A. Phillips Griffiths (Oxford: Oxford University Press, 1967), pp. 127-43.

3. The qualifying condition would have to be worked out more precisely if more than a rough account were required. For example, if the stakes were very high, a cautious gambler (one who "gambles" only when the stakes are small) could believe that *p* ("I will win") and yet decide not to bet because in cases in which the stakes are high he

demands virtual certainty. Perhaps it is generally true that the more one has at stake, the more favorable evidence or certainty one requires before acting. To put the point another way, it is perhaps generally true that if one has more at stake relative to p than to q one will require more evidence or certainty with respect to p than to q.

4. Alexander Bain, *The Emotions and the Will* (New York: D. Appleton & Co., 1876), p. 530.

5. Cf. Henry Haberly Price, "Belief 'In' and Belief 'That,'" *Religious Studies*, vol. 1, no. 1 (October, 1965), p. 16.

6. In order to communicate it would seem that there must be quite wide agreement on what counts as evidence for many propositions. For example, S's seeing a chair ahead, it is widely held, counts as evidence for the truth of the proposition that there is a chair ahead. Of course, this evidence is defeasible. Other pieces of conflicting evidence could annul its evidential value. But, in general, sense perception or observation is a means of collecting evidence. The sciences are sophisticated extensions of sense perception. The scientific methodology devises effective ways of collecting such evidence and making inductive inferences from the data. Except for difficult cases—i.e., propositions for which we have no notion whether they are (to speak very loosely) analytic or synthetic—we generally know and agree what in principle counts as evidence for a proposition being considered.

7. Cf. John Locke, *An Essay Concerning Human Understanding*, Bk. IV, Chapters 15, 16, 19, ed. by A. D. Woozley (New York: The World Publishing Co., 1964), pp. 403-15; pp. 428-33.

8. William James, *The Will to Believe* (New York: Dover Publications Inc., 1956). pp. 23-29.

9. This thesis is, of course, controversial—and one that cannot be pursued here without losing sight of the primary objectives of our present investigation.

Chapter 4

1. Kant, *Critique of Pure Reason*, A805 = B833ff.
2. *Ibid.*, A631 = B659 - A642 = B670.
3. *Ibid.*, A806=B834.
4. *Ibid.*, A828 = B856.
5. Immanuel Kant, *Critique of Judgment*, trans. by J. H. Bernard (New York: Hafner, 1951), p. 301 footnote to the second edition.
6. Marcel's argument from hope, to be discussed in a later chapter, has this same limitation. If one truly lives without hopes of the type discussed by Marcel, he can consistently deny the conclusion of the metaphysical argument.
7. It is important to note that the notion of "believing" here is a different one from the notion of "believing" in the previous chapter on hope and belief.

8. *Critique of Pure Reason*, A822 = B850.

9. Allen W. Wood, *Kant's Moral Religion* (Ithaca, New York: Cornell University Press, 1970), p.16.

10. Cf. *Critique of Judgment*, pp. 324-25; *Critique of Pure Reason*, Bxxix.

11. *Critique of Judgment*, p. 324.

12. *Critique of Pure Reason*, A568 = B596 - A583 = B611.

13. *Ibid.*, A830 = B858.

14. *Critique of Judgment*, p. 325.

15. *Dynamics of Faith* (New York: Harper & Brothers, 1957), pp. 17-18.

16. Immanuel Kant, *Lecture on Ethics*, trans. by Louis Infield (New York: Harper & Row, 1963), p. 95.

17. *Critique of Pure Reason*, Bxxx.

18. Immanuel Kant, *Critique of Practical Reason*, trans. by Thomas Kingsmill Abbott (London: Longmans, 1909), p. 241.

19. *Ibid.*, p. 242.

20. Wallace I. Matson presents a similar argument in *The Existence of God* (Ithaca, New York: Cornell University Press, 1965), pp. 198-201.

21. Kant, *Lectures on Ethics*, p. 81.

22. Lewis White Beck, *A Commentary on Kant's "Critique of Practical Reason"* (Chicago: University of Chicago Press, 1960), pp. 244-45.

23. Leo Tolstoy, *A Confession, The Gospel in Brief and What I Believe* (London: Oxford University Press, 1940).

24. Anthony Flew, "Tolstoi and the Meaning of Life," *Ethics*, vol. 73 (1963), 110-18; Kurt Baier, *The Meaning of Life* (Canberra, 1957).

25. *The Phenomenon of Man* (New York: Harper Torchbooks, Harper & Row, Publishers, 1961), p. 231.

26. *The Phenomenon of Man*, p. 231.

27. *Proceedings of the Society for Psychical Research*, vol. I, pt. 182 (January, 1953), 1-25.

28. "Human Immortality" in *The Will to Believe and Other Essays in Popular Philosophy* (New York: Dover Publications, Inc,. 1956), p. 10.

29. "Human Immortality," pp. 10-18.

30. "Human Immortality," pp. 20-30.

31. Peter Geach in *God and the Soul* (London: Routledge & Kegan Paul, 1969) maintains not only that resurrection is a consistent notion but he goes on to say that "unless a man comes to life again by resurrection, he does not live again after death. At best some mental remnant of him would survive death . . ." (p. 28)

32. *The World as Will and Representation*, trans. by E. F. J. Payne (New York: Dover Publications, Inc.), Vol. I, p. 86.

33. *Ibid.*, Vol. I, pp. 87-88.

34. *Ibid.*,Vol. I, pp. 379 and 392.
35. *Ibid.*, Vol. I, p. 210.
36. *Ibid.*, Vol. II, p. 141.
37. *Ibid.*, Vol. II pp. 216-27.
38. Cf. Philip Rieff, *Freud: The Mind of the Moralist* (Garden City, N.Y.: Doubleday & Company, Inc., 1961), p. 323.
39. *The Future of an Illusion*, trans. by W. D. Robson-Scott (Garden City, N.Y.: Doubleday & Company, Inc., 1964), p. 81.
40. *Ibid.*, p. 51.
41. *Ibid.*, pp. 11-19.
42. *Ibid.*, p. 47.
43. *Ibid.*, pp. 52-53.
44. Søren Kierkegaard, *The Sickness Unto Death*, pp. 215-16.
45. *The Future of an Illusion*, p. 49.
46. *Ibid.*
47. The *Oxford English Dictionary* lists, among others, the following definitions of "illusion." "The fact or condition of being deceived or deluded by appearances, or an instance of this: a mental state involving the attribution of reality to what is unreal; a false conception or idea; a deception, delusion, fancy." "The action, or an act of deceiving the bodily eye by false or unreal appearances, or the mental eye by false prospects, statements, etc.; deception, delusion, befooling."
48. *The Double Helix* (New York: A Mentor Book, New American Library, 1969).
49. *Personal Knowledge* (New York: Harper Torchbooks, Harper & Row, Publishers, 1964), p. 18. Others including Norwood Hanson, *Patterns of Discovery* (Cambridge: At the University Press, 1965) and Thomas Kuhn, *The Structure of Scientific Revolutions* (Chicago: The University of Chicago Press, 1962) have supported Polanyi's contention.
50. *Personal Knowledge*, pp. 15-16.
51. *Ibid.*, p. 143.
52. *Ibid.*, p. 65.
53. William James, "Is Life Worth Living?" in *The Will to Believe* (New York: Dover Publications, Inc., 1956), pp. 55-56.
54. Jean-Paul Sartre, "Existentialism is a Humanism," in *Existentialism from Dostoevsky to Sartre*, ed. by Walter Kaufmann (New York: The World Publishing Co., 1956), p. 299.
55. Albert Camus, *The Rebel*, trans. by Anthony Bower (New York: Knopf, 1957), p. 29.
56. *Ibid.*, p. 30.
57. *Ibid.*, p. 31.
58. *The Myth of Sisyphus*, trans. by Justin O'Brien (New York: Vintage Books, Random House, 1955), p. 7.
59. *Ibid.*, p. 37.
60. *Ibid.*, p. 39.

61. *Ibid.*, p. 38.
62. *Ibid.*, p. 5.
63. *Ibid.*, p. 41.
64. *Ibid.*, p. 50.
65. *Ibid.*, p. 13.
66. James, "Is Life Worth Living?" in *The Will to Believe*, p. 40.
67. *Ibid.*, p. 41.
68. *Ibid.*, p. 44.
69. Friedrich Nietzsche, *The Gay Science*, Bk. V, sec. 343, *The Portable Nietzsche*, trans. and ed. by Walter Kaufmann (New York: The Viking Press, 1954), pp. 447-48.
70. *Thus Spoke Zarathustra, Second Part, The Portable Nietzsche*, p. 198.
71. *The Will to Power*, trans. by Walter Kaufmann and R. J. Hollingdale (New York: Vintage Books, 1968), pp. 376-77.
72. *Twilight of the Idols*, in *The Portable Nietzsche*, pp. 500-501.
73. *The Antichrist*, sec. 18, in *The Portable Nietzsche*, p. 585.
74. *Ecce Homo*, trans. and ed. by Walter Kaufmann, (New York: Vintage Books, 1967), pp. 256.
75. *The Portable Nietzsche*, p. 97.
76. Ernst Bloch, *Das Prinzip Hoffnung* (Frankfurt am Main: Suhrkamp, 1959), p. 15. ("volles Leben")
77. *Ibid.*, p. 1616. ("vollkommenen Leben")
78. *Ibid.*, p. 1162. ("der Welt ohne Enttäuschung")
79. *Ibid.*, p. 680. ("Friede, Freiheit, Brot")
80. *Ibid.*, p. 368. ("Höchtes Gut")
81. Bloch, p. 16. (Bloch says: "Dieser Weg ist und bleibt der des Sozialismus, er ist die Praxis der konkreten Utopie. Alles an den Hoffnungsbildern Nicht-Illusionäre, Real-Mögliche geht zu Marx, arbeitet— wie immer jeweils variiert, situationsgemäss rationiert—in der sozialistischen Weltveranderung.")
82. *Ibid.*, p. 16. (Bloch says: "Die Träume vom besseren Leben, in ihnen war immer schon eine Glückswerdung erfragt, die erst der Marxismus eroffnen kann.")
83. Bloch, p. 1383. ("Kraut gegen den Tod") (Bloch says: "Und diese Gewissheit des Klassenbewusstseins, individuelle Fortdauer ist sich aufhebend, ist in der Tat ein Novum gegen den Tod." p. 1380)
84. If knowledge is gained by revelation, it may be that there is immediate recognition of the truth of revealed propositions. It is not my intention to rule such possibilities out. I am interested, rather, in seeing how far we may proceed without appealing to revelation. In traditional terms, I wish to work within the bounds of natural theology, without presupposing or precluding the possibility of revealed theology.
85. James, "The Will to Believe," in *The Will to Believe*, p. 18.
86. Cf. James, "Is Life Worth Living?" p. 55.
87. "The Will to Believe," pp. 26-27.

88. James, "The Sentiment of Rationality," in *The Will to Believe*, p. 109.

89. This phrase is taken from an interesting, and in some ways similar, argument by Blaise Pascal in *Pensees* (233), trans, by W. F. Trotter (New York: E. P. Dutton & Co., Inc., 1958), p. 68.

90. I say, "appears to accept the principle" because, later, I shall offer an interpretation of James which does not require the principle.

91. "The Will to Believe," p. 11.

92. "Is Life Worth Living?" p. 54.

93. "The Will to Believe," pp. 29-30.

94. The criterion of justified hope helps one in seeking the truth, by keeping certain possibilities open (even remote ones) which one would not, if he merely followed the maxim to avoid error. By keeping these possibilities open, one is in a good position to look for, and discover, the truth of propositions which would otherwise have remained unknown.

95. *Ibid.*, pp. 1-2 (underlines mine).

96. "The Sentiment of Rationality," p. 90.

97. *Ibid.*, pp. 109-110.

98. "Is Life Worth Living?" p. 62.

99. "The Will to Believe," p. 29.

100. "Is Life Worth Living?" p. 57.

101. *Ibid.*, pp. 57-58.

102. *Ibid.*, p. 56.

103. *Athens and Jerusalem*, trans. by Bernard Martin (New York: Simon and Schuster, 1968), pp. 396-97.

Chapter 5

1. Cf. Gabriel Marcel, *Metaphysical Journal*, trans. by Bernard Wall (Chicago: Henry Regnery Co., 1952), p. 97.

2. *Ibid.*, p. 96.

3. *Mystery of Being*, vol. II, pp. 86-87

4. Ibid., p. 89.

5. Marcel holds that the calculation of probability is, in the special cases he examined, incompatible with hope. The arguments of Marcel and Kierkegaard to be discussed here press a related point. I have argued, on the other hand, that the calculation of probability is not actually incompatible with holding such hopes; it simply does not, and ought not, play a very large role in the context of relevant hopes. Other considerations take due precedence. Hence the parallel to be drawn between experiences of hope and religious faith need not affect the issue. Calculations of probability are simply not crucial, and need not be.

6. *Concluding Unscientific Postscript*, trans. by David F. Swenson and Walter Lowrie (Princeton: Princeton University Press, 1941), p. 30.

7. *C. U. P.*, p. 41.

8. *C. U. P.*, p. 189.

9. *C. U. P.*, p. 190.

10. Kierkegaard, *Concluding Unscientific Postscript*, p. 180.

11. Søren Kierkegaard, *The Journals of Kierkegaard,* trans. by Alexander Dru (New York: Harper & Row, 1958), p. 185.

12. *Concluding Unscientific Postscript*, p. 182.

13. *Ibid.*, p. 188.

14. *Ibid.*, p. 407.

15. *Ibid.*, p. 406.

16. *Ibid.*, p. 453.

17. *Ibid.*, p. 406.

18. *Ibid.*, p. 182.

19. Cf. James, "The Sentiment of Rationality," p. 63.

20. *Ibid.*, p. 64.

21. *Concluding Unscientific Postscript*, p. 382.

22. *Ibid.*, p. 355.

23. *Ibid.*, p. 380.

24. *Ibid.*, p. 349 footnote.

25. *Varieties of Religious Experience* (New York: A Mentor Book. The New American Library, 1958), Lectures XI-XV, pp. 207-291.

26. Miguel de Unamuno, *Tragic Sense of Life*, trans. by J. E. Crawford Flitch (New York: Dover Publications, Inc., 1954), p. 186.

27. *Ibid.*, p. 194.

28. *Ibid.*, p. 120.

29. Søren Kierkegaard, *Fear and Trembling* and *The Sickness Unto Death* (Garden City, New York: Doubleday & Company, Inc., 1954), espec. pp. 49-64; pp. 86-91.

30. Although Wittgenstein's position is in many ways very different from Kierkegaard's, in *Concluding Unscientific Postscript*, there is a definite affinity if not a direct influence. In *Ludwig Wittgenstein: A Memoir* (Oxford: Oxford University Press, 1958), Norman Malcolm reports that Wittgenstein held Kierkegaard in esteem. He notes that Wittgenstein referred to Kierkegaard "with something of awe in his expression, as a 'really religious' man. He had read the *Concluding Unscientific Postscript*—but found it 'too deep' for him" (p.71).

31. Ludwig Wittgenstein, *Lectures and Conversations on Aesthetics, Psychology and Religious Belief*, ed. by Cyril Barrett (Berkeley: University of California Press, 1967), p. 53.

32. *Ibid.*, p. 54.

33. *Ibid.*, p. 56.

34. *Ibid.*, p. 53.

35. *Ibid.*

36. Grammatically speaking, it may be that "belief"—in the religious context—is not a primitive term. The primitive may well be "religious-belief." If so, then the ordinary use of "belief" in other contexts cannot be shifted without adjustment or equivocation to the religious context.

37. *Ibid.*, pp. 59-60.

38. *Ibid.*, pp. 61-62.

39. The sort of analysis I have in mind may be found in R. M. Hare, "Theology and Falsification" in Antony Flew and Alasdaire MacIntyre, eds., *New Essays in Philosophical Theology* (London: S. C. M. Press, 1955), pp. 99-103; R. M. Hare, "Religion and Morals" in Basil Mitchell, ed., *Faith and Logic* (London: Allen & Unwin, 1957), pp. 176-193; R. B. Braithwaite, *An Empiricist's View of the Nature of Religious Belief* (Cambridge University Press, 1955).

40. As we saw above, it is unlikely that a religious believer would give up his religious-beliefs because of lack of evidence. As with giving up hope, a variety of personal and moral considerations combine to change one's attitude and/or relationship to the object of concern.

41. This analogy is an adaptation of Basil Mitchell's account of the parallel between a resistance fighter's relationship to a resistance leader and a believer's relationship to God. Mitchell offers the analogy in resolving the falsifiability problem so widely discussed some years ago in *New Essays in Philosophical Theology*, ed. by Antony Flew and Alasdaire MacIntyre (London: SCM Press Ltd., 1963), pp. 103-105.

Chapter 6

1. Jürgen Moltmann, *Theology of Hope*, p. 11

2. "On the Ontological Mystery," p. 16.

3. On R. B. Braithwaite's account of models in scientific explanation, the status of the theological model is similar to that of the scientific model. In *Scientific Explanation* (Cambridge, England: At the University Press, 1968), p. 93, Braithwaite says that "thinking of scientific theories by means of models is always *as-if* thinking."

4. Again, there is a parallel here between thinking *via* the theological model and thinking *via* a scientific model. Speaking of scientific models, Max Black says, "We pin our hopes upon the existence of a common structure in both fields." Max Black, *Models and Metaphors* (Ithaca, New York: Cornell University Press, 1962), p. 238.

5. *Athens and Jerusalem*, p. 69.

6. *Cosmos and History* (New York: Harper & Row Publishers, 1959), pp. 161-162.

7. Søren Kierkegaard, *Purity of Heart is to Will One Thing* (New York: Harper & Row, Publishers, 1956). In part, this is what Kierkegaard has in mind when he speaks of the need for infinite resignation on

the part of the religious person. This kind of resignation is distinct from that advocated by Stoicism.

8. *Hope in Time of Abandonment*, pp. 248-249.

9. Moltmann, *Theology of Hope*, pp. 1-342.

10. C. F. D. Moule, *The Meaning of Hope*, Facet Book (Philadelphia: Fortress Press, 1963), pp. 1-55.

11. Genesis 12:2; 15:5.

12. Gen. 17:4.

13. Cf. Psalms 23 & 27.

14. Proverbs 10:28; 11:7; Isaiah 32:17.

15. Jeremiah 14:19; Isa. 59:11; Job 30:26.

16. Jer. 30 & 31; Isa. 41; Ezekiel 38 & 39.

17. Cf. e.g., Matthew 12:21.

18. Matt. 25:31.

19. Cf. e.g., Matt. 22:23; Acts 23:6; 24:15.

20. Cf. Hebrews 6:17-20.

21. II Timothy 4:18; I Corinthians 15:19.

22. Romans 4:12.

23. Cf. Rom. 5:15.

24. Rom. 4:16-25.

25. Rom. 8:22-25.

26. Rom. 8:38-39. (R. S. V.)

27. I Cor. 15:58. (R. S. V.)

28. The possibility that, through a private revelation or a beatific vision, one could become certain of his own salvation cannot be ruled out. But the alternative has limited application at best. Revelations and visions cannot (and even biblically, could not) but be rare occurrences.

29. *Summa Theologiae*, 2a2ae. 18, 4.

30. *Ibid.*, 2a2ae. 18, 2.

31. *Ibid.*, 2a2ae. 17, 7.

32. *Ibid.*

33. *Ibid.*

34. *Ibid.*, 2a2ae. 20 & 21.

35. *Ibid.*, 2a2ae. 20, 1.

36. *Ibid.*, 2a2ae. 21, 1.

37. John Calvin, *Institute of the Christian Religion*, ed. by John T. McNeill, trans. by Ford Lewis Battles (2 vols.; Philadelphia: The Westminster Press, 1960), III, 39.

38. *Ibid.*, 39-40; III, 24, 1.

39. *Ibid.*, III, 40.

40. Cf. *Ibid.*, II, 10.3; and Edward A. Dowey, Jr., *The Knowledge of God in Calvin's Theology* (New York: Columbia University Press, 1952), p. 191.

41. *Ibid.*, 2.42.

42. Emil Brunner, *The Christian Doctrine of the Church, Faith, and the Consummation*, trans. by David Cairns and T. H. L. Parker, (Philadelphia: The Westminster Press, 1960), p. 345.

43. *Concluding Unscientific Postcript*, p. 515.

44. Kierkegaard says: "Religiousness A must first be present in the individual before there can be any question of becoming aware of the dialectic of B." *Ibid.*, p. 494.

45. *Ibid.*, p. 497.

46. *Ibid.*, p. 510.

47. *Ibid.*, p. 191.

48. *Ibid.*, p. 502.

49. *Ibid.*, p. 504.

50. Jacques Ellul, *Hope in Time of Abandonment*, trans. by C. Edward Hopkin (New York: The Seabury Press, 1973), p. 222.

Selected Bibliography

Aquinas, Thomas. *Summa Theologiae,* 1a2ae. 40-48. *Fear and Anger,* vol. 21. Translated and edited by John Patrick Reid O.P. London: Blackfriars, 1965.

Aquinas, Thomas. *Summa Theologiae,* 2a2ae. 17-22. *Hope,* vol. 33. Translated and edited by William J. Hill O.P. London: Blackfriars, 1966.

Bain, Alexander. *The Emotions and the Will.* New York: D. Appleton & Co., 1876.

Beardslee, William A. *A House for Hope: A Study in Process and Biblical Thought.* Philadelphia: Westminster Press, 1972.

Beck, Lewis White. *A Commentary on Kant's 'Critique of Pratical Reason.'* Chicago: University of Chicago Press, 1960.

Bloch, Ernst. *Das Prinzip Hoffnung.* Frankfurt am Main: Suhrkamp, 1959.

Boden, Margaret. "Optimism," *Philosophy,* vol. 41 (1966).

Braaten, Carl E. *The Future of God: The Revolutionary Dynamics of Hope.* New York: Harper & Row, 1969.

Brunner, Emil. *The Christian Doctrine of the Church, Faith, and the Consummation.* Translated by David Cairns and T. H. L. Parker. Philadelphia: The Westminster Press, 1960.

Brunner, Emil. *Faith, Hope, and Love.* Philadelphia: Westminster Press, 1956.

Bultmann, Rudolf, and Karl Rengstorf. *Hope.* Translated by Dorothea M. Barton and edited by P. R. Ackroyd. London: A. & C. Black, 1963.

Calvin, John. *Institutes of the Christian Religion.* Edited by John T. McNeill. Translated by Ford Lewis Battles. 2 vols. Philadelphia: The Westminster Press, 1960.

Camus, Albert. *The Myth of Sisyphus*. Translated by Justin O'Brien. New York: Knopf, 1955.

Camus, Albert, *The Rebel*. Translated by Anthony Bower. New York: Knopf, 1957.

Capps, Walter, editor. *The Future of Hope*. Philadelphia: Fortress Press, 1970.

Capps, Walter H. *Time Invades the Cathedral: Tension in the School of Hope*. Philadelphia: Fortress Press, 1972.

Cousins, Ewert, editor. *Hope and the Future of Man*. Philadelphia: Fortress Press, 1972.

Day, J. P. "The Anatomy of Hope and Fear," *Mind,* vol. LXXIX (July, 1970).

Day, J. P. "Hope," *American Philosophical Quarterly,* vol. VI, no. 2 (April, 1969).

Descartes, Rene. *The Passions of the Soul. The Philosophical Works of Descartes.* Translated by Elizabeth S. Haldene and G. R. T. Ross. Vol. II Cambridge, England: At the University Press, 1968.

Eliade, Mircea. *Cosmos and History*. New York: Harper & Row, Publishers, 1959.

Ellul, Jacques. *Hope in Time of Abandonment*. Translated by C. Edward Hopkin. New York: Seabury Press, 1973.

Flew, Antony, and Alasdair NacIntyre. *New Essays in Philosophical Theology*. London: S. C. M. Press, Ltd., 1963.

Freud, Sigmund. *The Future of an Illusion*. Translated by W. D. Robson-Scott. Garden City, New York: Doubleday & Company, Inc., 1964.

Herzog, Frederick, editor. *The Future of Hope*. New York: Herder and Herder, 1970.

Hinton, J. M. "Hoping and Wishing," *Proceedings of the Aristotelian Society,* Supplementary Volume 44, 1970.

Hobbes, Thomas. *Leviathan*. Indianapolis: The Bobbs-Merrill Company, Inc., 1958.

Hume, David. *A Treatise of Human Nature*. Edited by L. A. Selby-Bigge. Oxford: At the Clarendon Press, 1888.

James, William. *Varieties of Religious Experience*. New York: A Mentor Book. The New American Library, 1958.

James, William. *The Will to Believe*. New York: Dover Publications, Inc., 1956.

Kant, Immanuel. *Critique of Judgment*. Translated by J. H. Bernard. New York: Hafner, 1951.

Kant, Immanuel. *Critique of Practical Reason*. Translated by Thomas Kingsmill Abbott. London: Longmans, 1909.

Kant, Immanuel. *Critique of Pure Reason.* Translated by Norman Kemp Smith. New York: St. Martin's Press, 1965.

Kant, Immanuel. *Lectures on Ethics.* Translated by Louis Infield. New York: Harper & Row, 1963.

Kierkegaard, Søren. *Concluding Unscientific Postscript.* Translated by David F. Swenson and Walter Lowrie. Princeton: Princeton University Press, 1941.

Kierkegaard, Søren. *Fear and Trembling* and *The Sickness Unto Death.* Translated by Walter Lowrie. Garden City, New York: Doubleday & Company, Inc., 1954.

Kierkegaard, Søren. *The Journals of Kierkegaard.* Translated by Alexander. New York: Harper & Row, 1958.

Kierkegaard, Søren. *Purity of Heart Is to Will One Thing.* Translated by Douglas Steere. New York: Harper & Row, 1956.

Locke, John. *An Essay Concerning Human Understanding.* New York: The World Publishing Co., 1964.

Marcel, Gabriel. *Being and Having: An Existentialist Diary.* Translated by Katherine Farrer. New York: Harper & Row, 1965.

Marcel, Gabriel. *Homo Viator.* Translated by Emma Crawfurd. New York: Harper & Row, 1962.

Marcel, Gabriel. *Methaphysical Journal.* Translated by Bernard Wall. Chicago: Henry Regnery Co., 1952.

Marcel, Gabriel. *Mystery of Being.* Vol. II: *Faith and Reality.* Translated by Rene Hague. Chicago: Henry Regnery Co., 1960.

Marcel, Gabriel. "On the Ontological Mystery." *The Philosophy of Existence.* London: The Harvill Press, 1948.

Marcel, Gabriel. *Searchings.* New York: Newman Press, 1967.

Marty, Martin E., and Dean G. Peerman, editors. *New Theology,* no.5. New York: The Macmillan Company, 1968.

Meeks, M. Douglas. *Origins of the Theology of Hope.* Philadelphia: Fortress Press, 1974.

Mill, John Stuart. *Theism.* Edited by Richard Taylor. Indianapolis: The Bobbs-Merrill Co., Inc., 1957.

Moltmann, Jürgen. *The Experiment Hope.* Translated by M. Douglas Meeks. Philadelphia: Fortress Press, 1975.

Moltman, Jürgen. *Theology of Hope: On the Ground and the Implications of a Christian Eschatology.* New York: Harper & Row, 1967.

Moule, C. F. D. *The Meaning of Hope.* Facet Book. Philadelphia: Fortress Press, 1963.

Nietzsche, Friedrich. *Ecce Homo.* Translated and edited by Walter Kaufmann. New York: Vintage Books, 1967.

Nietzsche, Friedrich. *The Portable Nietzsche.* Translated and edited by Walter Kaufmann. New York: The Viking Press, 1954.

Nietzsche, Friedrich. *The Will to Power.* Translated by Walter Kaufmann and R. J. Hollingdale. New York: Vintage Books, 1968.

Polanyi, Michael. *Personal Knowledge.* New York: Harper & Row, Publishers, 1964.

Price, H. H. "Belief 'In' and Belief 'That,'" *Religious Studies,* vol. 1, no. 1 (October, 1965).

Radford, Colin. "Hoping and Wishing," *Proceedings of the Aristotelian Society,* Supplementary Volume 44, 1970.

Radford, Colin. "Hoping, Wishing, and Dogs," *Inquiry,* vol. 13, no. 1 (Spring, 1970).

Schopenhauer, Arthur. *The World As Will and Representation.* Translated by E. F. J. Payne. New York: Dover Publications, Inc., 1969.

Shestov, Lev. *Athens and Jerusalem.* Translated by Bernard Martin. New York: Simon and Schuster, 1968.

Teilhard de Chardin, Pierre. *The Phenomenon of Man.* Translated by Bernard Wall. New York: Harper & Row, 1961.

Thomson, James Sutherland. *The Hope of the Gospel.* London: S. C. M. Press, 1955.

Tillich, Paul. *Dynamics of Faith.* New York: Harper & Row, Publishers, 1958.

Tolstoy, Leo. *A Confession, The Gospel in Brief and What I Believe.* London: Oxford University Press, 1940.

Unamuno, Miguel de. *Tragic Sense of Life.* Translated by J. E. Crawford Flitch. New York: Dover Publications, Inc., 1954.

Wheatley, J. M. O. "Wishing and Hoping," *Analysis,* vol. 18, no. 6 (June, 1958).

Wittgenstein, Ludwig. *Lectures and Conversations on Aesthetics, Psychology and Religious Belief.* Edited by Cyril Barrett. Berkeley: University of California Press, 1967.

Zimmerli, Walther. *Man and His Hope in the Old Testament.* London: S. C. M. Press, 1971.

Index